MILLER'S
ANTIQUES
& COLLECTABLES

MILLER'S
ANTIQUES
& COLLECTABLES
The Facts At Your Fingertips

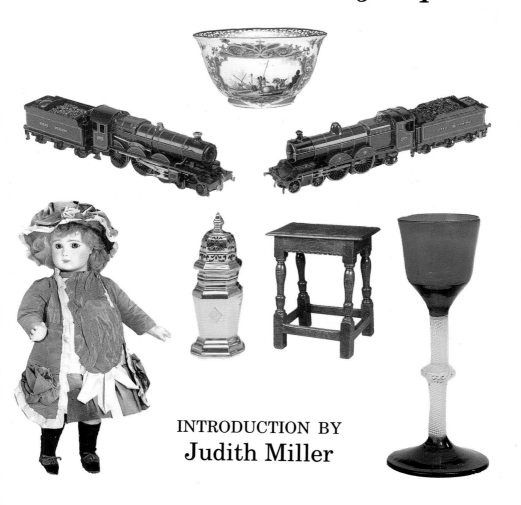

INTRODUCTION BY
Judith Miller

Miller's Antiques and Collectables
The Facts at Your Fingertips

First published in Great Britain in 1993 by Miller's,
an imprint of Mitchell Beazley, both imprints of
Octopus Publishing Group Limited
2-4 Heron Quays, London E14 4JP
© 1993 Octopus Publishing Group Limited
Reprinted 1993,1995, 1996, 1997, 1998, 1999
Miller's is a registered trademark of Octopus Publishing Group Limited

Editor Janet Gleeson
Art Editor Prue Bucknall
Special Photography Jacqui Hurst
Executive Art Editor John Grain
Production Fiona Wright
Indexer Hilary Bird
Art Director Tim Foster
Senior Executive Editor Frances Gertler

A CIP catalogue record for this book is available from
the British Library
ISBN 1 85732 179 0

Set in Bembo
Produced by Toppan Printing Co., (H.K.) Ltd.
Printed and bound in Hong Kong

cover pictures: an Ibanez Musician electric bass guitar belonging to John Entwistle; a Meissen *famille verte* dish plate, c1730, a Clarice Cliff teapot, c1935; a *cloisonné* carriage clock, c1870, a Merrythought teddy bear, c1930; a 17thC English walnut chest weight, an 18thC mahogany longcase clock by Samuel Guy, a pair of ruby slippers worn by Judy Garland, a 19thC French bracket clock, a Moorcroft baluster vase c1928, a 19thC Staffordshire pottery Toby Jug, an early 19thC yew armchair, a George III soup tureen and cover c1770, an 18thC mahogany bureau, a 19thC kazak rug, a Meissen slop bowl, c1730, two gauge 0 electric locomotives with pick-ups c1940, a Jules Steiner bisque doll, c1890, a silver caster by Matthew Cooper, c1703, a 17thC oak joint stool, a two-colour opaque twist wine glass c1765.

picture pages 1 & 2: a 19thC William de Morgan two-handled vase, William IV silver gilt dessert-spoons, 18thC Meissen porcelain figures, a Baccarat rose paper-

CONTENTS

INTRODUCTION

People become interested in antiques and collectables for a variety of reasons. In my own case there was nothing in my background to suggest that I would – my parents had none. Indeed, my mother was of a generation which, for the most part, used to discard everything once it was old. However, as an impoverished student living in a run-down part of Edinburgh during the late 1960s I bought a few cheap, pretty plates from the local junk shops that I passed every day on my way to and from the university. To me they provided a far more attractive and unusual means of decorating the walls of my room than the posters favoured by my flatmates. In much the same way as many other people who inherit or buy the odd item of china or furniture, I then became increasingly intrigued as to when and where the plates had been made. Later still, I also became interested in their value. Were they now worth more than I paid for them?

While my first foray into the world of antiques did not realize any profit to speak of, this in no way detracted from the considerable enjoyment my purchases gave me. Indeed, over the subsequent years, almost every collector I have met has bought for pleasure rather than profit; the value of any particular piece usually being a side issue to the joys of researching it, tracking it down, buying it, holding or looking at it, showing it off and even the simple fact of owning it.

Nevertheless, during a period in which buying and selling shares on the stock market has sometimes been a bit like swapping deck chairs on the *Titanic*, antiques and collectables have, for the most part, proved to be a good investment. This is undoubtedly one of the main reasons for the enormous ground swell of interest in the subject over the last decade. Moreover, the prospect of finding a long-forgotten object gathering dust in the attic, or buying for a few pounds an insignificant-looking item at a car boot sale that at auction turns out to be worth a small fortune, lends to this fascinating leisure activity all the excitement of a treasure hunt.

People often ask me, how they can learn about antiques. Although there is no magic way of becoming an expert overnight, there's no great mystery to it either. Learning about antiques is great fun and the best way of going about it is to do what I did: visit museums and stately homes, read books and attend courses on the subject, look around antiques shops, markets, fairs and auctions and, above all, ask questions.

Museums and stately homes are a great place to start. Invariably they contain some of the finest examples of all manner of antiques and thus help you to get your eye in and learn when a piece looks right. However, don't try and take in too much at once. You'll learn far more quickly if you concentrate on one subject at a time.

There are numerous books on antiques and collectables available today – many more than when I first became interested. The *Miller's Price Guides* and *Checklists*, for example, are particularly useful! Containing thousands of pictures of antiques they give you a pretty good idea of current prices and help to familiarize you with the language of antiques. Courses run by leading auctioneers, such as Christie's and Sotheby's, or local education departments are also now widely available and offer expert tuition in a particular subject. If you do decide to attend one, don't feel embarrassed about asking questions. I remember attending a weekend course on porcelain run by Geoffrey Godden a few years ago. Right at the end a man suddenly confessed he had been confused by much of what had been said over the two days; he didn't understand the continual references to hard- and soft-paste porcelain, or what the difference was between them – a crucial piece of information that could have been easily explained if only he had asked at the outset.

Many people also feel intimidated about striking up a conversation with a dealer when visiting a shop, antique fair or market. However, as I have found over the years, this is one of the best ways of acquiring knowledge. Indeed, most dealers are only too happy to discuss a piece and answer a reasonable number of questions. But do be sensitive to the fact that dealers have to make a living. Pick a quiet moment when they're not busy.

Attending auctions, which are held once a week or fortnight in most parts of the country, gives you the opportunity to view an enormous range of antiques and also introduces you to the real nitty-gritty of buying and selling.

Go to the sale previews, buy a catalogue and, if you are particularly interested in a piece, ask to see someone from the auction house and discuss factors such as its history, any damage and the estimated price. Also go along to the sale itself, even if you have no intention of buying, and write down on the catalogue the prices pieces fetch as they go under the hammer. By doing this you will be able to compare estimates with realized prices, and gradually build up a feel for how the market is doing in particular areas.

By the time you have done all or most of the above you will have acquired a considerable amount of knowledge about the antiques you have become interested in. However, do bear in mind that we are not talking about an exact science here. For every rule there is an exception. For example, I once wrote an article confidently stating that all 18th-century sideboards had six legs. When this appeared in print it was accompanied by a number of illustrations, one of which showed a totally authentic piece with four legs! I have also heard three eminent experts in their field disagree vehemently over the authenticity of a piece of oak furniture. This is not an unusual occurrence and is very much part of the joy of antiques.

On a slightly more serious note, I've also seen so-called 'antique' furniture made up by modern craftsmen using old wood and traditional techniques. Some pieces are so well done it's virtually impossible to distinguish between the fake and an original. As someone once pointed out to me: there are more English oak refectory tables distributed around the world than there were houses in 16th-century England of a sufficient size to even get them in the front door. So, do be careful, especially if you are thinking of paying a lot of money for something. Most antiques dealers are both honest and honourable, but as in most spheres of business, there are exceptions.

The questions I am most often asked are: how much is something worth, or how much should I pay for it? Well, price is almost always determined by a combination of four factors: condition, age, rarity and desirability. Condition can be vital. After a pristine Steiff teddy bear went for £55,000 at Sotheby's a few years ago, Bond Street was inundated with gentlemen in pinstripe suits clutching their play-worn childhood companions. There was considerable disappointment when they were informed that they were, at best, only worth £50-£100. Age is also obviously important, as the older something is the greater the likelihood few examples will have survived. However, the rarity of a piece does not guarantee desirability, and it is the latter that is the most important factor in determining the price something will fetch. For example, Roman glass is old, can be found in good condition and some pieces are quite rare. However, if it is not considered desirable it will sell for a very low price at auction. In other words, the old adage that a piece is only worth what two people are prepared to pay for it usually holds good.

Assessing the value of an antique or a collectable is more difficult in some areas than others. For example, a good quality 19th-century mahogany dining table and chairs by a well-known maker can be said to have an intrinsic value. Precedent says they will at least have held their value 10 years on. Much the same can be said for pieces of 18th-century porcelain or silverware. However, it is far more difficult to predict whether a 1950s Japanese plastic robot, a smashed-up Fender guitar once played by Jimi Hendrix (one recently fetched £35,000 at auction) or a John Paul Gaultier dress designed for Madonna will be worth in 30 years time the sort of sums of money the present generation are prepared to pay for them. Of course, trying to predict these things is very much part of the fun of collecting – provided, that is, you stick to the following rules: always buy the best piece you can afford, especially in terms of condition and rarity. Never buy anything you don't like or you can't live with – you may have to live with it for a long time before you can get your money back. In fact, as long as you know what you're buying and the price you pay is appropriate at the time, you probably won't go far wrong.

JUDITH MILLER

The values given in this book for featured objects reflect the sort of prices you might expect to pay for similar pieces at an auction-house or a dealer. As there are so many variable factors involved in the pricing of antiques, the values should be used only as a general guide.

PERIODS & STYLES

DATES	BRITISH MONARCH	UK PERIOD	FRENCH PERIOD	GERMAN PERIOD	US PERIOD	STYLE
1558–1603	Elizabeth I	Elizabethan	Renaissance			Gothic
1603–1625	James I	Jacobean		Renaissance (to c1650)		
1625–1649	Charles I	Caroleon	Louis XIII (1610–1643)		Early Colonial	Baroque (c1620–1700)
1649–1660	Commonwealth	Cromwellian	Louis XIV (1643–1715)	Renaissance/ Baroque (c1650–1700)		
1660–1685	Charles II	Restoration				
1685–1689	James II	Restoration				
1689–1694	William & Mary				William & Mary	
1694–1702	William III	William III			Dutch Colonial	Rococo (c1695–1760)
1702–1714	Anne	Queen Anne		Baroque (c1700–1730)	Queen Anne	
1714–1727	George I	Early Georgian	Régence (1715–1723)		Chippendale	(from 1760)
1727–1760	George II	Early Georgian	Louis XV (1723–1774)	Rococo		
1760–1811	George III	Late Georgian	Louis XVI (1774–1793)	Neoclassicism (c1760–1800)		Neoclassical (c1755–1805)
			Directoire (1793–1799)		Early Federal (1790–1810)	
			Empire (1799–1815)	Empire (c1800–1815)	American Directoire (1798–1804)	Empire (c1799–1815)
					American Empire (1804–1815)	
1812–1820	George III	Regency	Restauration (1815–1830)	Biedermeier (c1815–1848)	Later Federal (1810–1830)	Regency (c1812–1930)
1820–1830	George IV	Regency				
1830–1837	William IV	William IV	Louis Philippe (1830–1848)	Revivale (c1830–1880)		Eclectic (c1830–1880)
1837–1901	Victoria	Victorian	2nd Empire (1848–1870)		Victorian	
			3rd Republic (1871–1940)	Jugendstil (c1880–1920)	Art Nouveau (c1900–1920)	Arts & Crafts (1880–1900)
1901–1910	Edward VII	Edwardian				Art Nouveau (c1900–1920)

PART 1

WHERE

TO BEGIN

AUCTIONS

Auctions are one of the most exciting ways in which to buy antiques. Here you will find almost every type of collectable; from objects worth millions, to boxes of bric-a-brac costing just a few pounds. But buying at auction is very different from buying in a shop or market, and can seem quite bewildering to anyone who has never visited a saleroom or bought in this way before. Auctions are not limited to the big city salerooms. The London branches of famous firms such as Sotheby's, Christie's, Phillips and Bonhams may account for the vast majority of more expensive antiques sold at auction in this country, but they also have provincial branches and there is a network of local auctioneers throughout the country where you can often buy less expensive antiques and bric-a-brac, provided you are willing to sift through the varied goods on offer to find whatever it is you are looking for.

Most would-be collectors who overcome

BUYING AT AUCTION
- **BUY THE CATALOGUE**
- **VIEW THE SALE VERY THOROUGHLY**
- **DECIDE ON YOUR PRICE LIMIT AND STICK TO IT**

---

their initial misgivings and visit an auction for the first time, find themselves hooked on the exciting atmosphere of the saleroom. The large turnover of goods means that there is always a possibility of uncovering an undiscovered treasure – or "sleeper" as it is known in the trade – and provided certain basic guidelines are followed, auctions are still one of the best places to buy reasonably-priced objects of good quality.

Going to auctions regularly is also an excellent way of learning about your area of interest before beginning to collect. If you attend saleroom previews regularly and read catalogues carefully, you will soon acquire a sound knowledge and a feel for prices which will stand you in good stead when you begin to spend money on your collection.

BUYING AT AUCTION
CATALOGUES

Before every sale is held, the saleroom will identify the goods to be sold in a catalogue. Whether it's a typed sheet or a glossy illustrated publication, it will list and number the objects in the order in which they will be sold. The numbers in the catalogue, known as "lot" numbers, correspond to those attached to each object or "lot".

Next to each catalogue entry there may be a suggested price range, for example £50-80. These figures show the price the auction house valuer expects the object to fetch, and are known as the "estimate". If there are no estimates printed in the catalogue they may be pinned up in the saleroom, if not, ask the auctioneer. Estimates should only ever be taken as a rough guide,

Some lots contain more than one item, all these albums were sold together in a stamp sale.

they are never a guarantee of the price for which something will be sold. Ultimately any work of art, no matter how rare or valuable, is only worth at auction what two or more people are willing to bid for it, and it is this element of uncertainty that gives auctions their special appeal.

VIEWING THE SALE

About two or three days before the day of the sale, all the objects to be sold will be put on display, so that buyers can examine them; this is known as the "view" or "sale preview". It's very important to attend one of these preview days because on the morning of the sale, when the porters are getting everything ready for selling, it may be impossible to view properly.

At the preview you will notice that every object has been marked with its lot number which corresponds to the number in your catalogue. Objects are rarely displayed in numerical order, so if something sounded fascinating in the catalogue and you can't find it at the view, ask one of the saleroom staff to help you. That way you won't miss anything which has been badly displayed.

At larger auction houses pay careful attention to the wording of the catalogue entry. Read the explanations at the beginning of the catalogue, which tell you the signifi-

cance of words such as "attributed to", "style of", and "after". This catalogue terminology is like a code which tells you the valuer's opinion of the date and authenticity of a piece and will have an important bearing on its value. Ask to speak to the expert in charge of the sale if you would like more information about a particular piece.

Always examine very, very thoroughly any object on which you intend to bid, and make up your own mind as to its authenticity. Pay particular attention to the condition of the piece and take into account the cost of restoration, which may be considerable, before deciding on your bidding limit. Also bear in mind that an auctioneer's commission (usually 10%–15% of the hammer price – the price at which the object is sold in the saleroom) and VAT on the commission, will usually be added to the hammer price.

Above Each lot should be clearly marked with a number.
Right Viewing before the auction takes place.

An auction of silver in progress.

BIDDING

If after viewing the sale, you decide you might want to bid, find out if you need to register first. Some salerooms will want you to fill in a form with your name, address and phone number before the sale; some issue you with a number to hold up should your bid be successful; in others you simply call out your name and fill in a form at the time.

If you are not paying in cash, ask whether a cheque or credit card will be acceptable as a method of payment. If you intend to spend a large sum of money you may have to supply bank references.

Some sales last for several hours; if the lots which interest you are towards the end of the sale and you don't want to sit through the whole auction, find out how many lots the auctioneer sells per hour (usually about 100) to work out roughly when your lot will be sold; but remember to allow yourself a bit of extra time so you don't arrive too late.

If you can't get to the sale you can usually leave a bid with the commissions clerk, who will bid on your behalf.

When the sale begins, the auctioneer will call out each lot number to be sold and will start the bidding at a figure which is usually slightly below the lower estimate. As the people present signal to him by waving or nodding he will call out their bids in regular sums, called increments. Depending on the value of the piece, the bidding could rise in £5s, £10s, £20s, £100s, £1,000s, or more, the increments increasing as the price rises. The auctioneer will indicate that the bidding is finished by banging a small hammer, called a gavel, on the rostrum, and recording the sale and the name or number of the successful bidder. People who have never been to an auction before often worry that an ill-timed cough or sneeze could be mistaken as a bid and land them with a masterpiece; ask anyone with experience of auctions and they will tell you that this is unheard of.

When you are bidding for the first time remember to make your bids clearly and quickly. In a packed saleroom it can be quite difficult to attract the auctioneer's attention, so don't be faint hearted: wave your catalogue or bidding card and call out if need be. However, if the bidding is rising rapidly and the auctioneer seems to be ignoring you, don't worry; an auctioneer will usually only take bids from two people at a time, when one drops out he will look around the room for someone else to join in; if you are still within your limit that is your moment!

SELLING AT AUCTION

Taking a prized possession for sale at auction can seem every bit as daunting as buying; especially if you don't know the object's history or what it might be worth. You are, after all, taking along something you hope may be valuable, and quite possibly have treasured for a very long time. But although many would-be vendors are put off by the thought of rejection, auction houses offer a very useful way of finding out more about your property and their advice is nearly always absolutely free.

> ### SELLING AT AUCTION
> - TRY TO GET MORE THAN ONE VALUER'S OPINION
> - PHONE TO MAKE AN APPOINTMENT IF NECESSARY
> - AGREE ALL CHARGES BEFORE LEAVING YOUR PROPERTY FOR SALE
> - FIND OUT HOW SOON YOUR PROPERTY WILL BE SOLD

WHAT IT'S WORTH

When you visit one of the larger auction houses you will have to queue up and show your property to a receptionist who will decide which expert should be called to value it for you.

Before the auction house expert examines your property he (or she) will probably ask you for anything you can tell him about the object. The history of an object, known as its "provenance", can help enormously in its correct identification and valuation. Even details which might seem insignificant to you can help a valuer, so if you know your table once belonged to Aunt Ethel who lived in Devon and bought it from a local Duchess, then don't forget to say so.

After careful examination the valuer will probably tell you what he can about your object. This may be where, when and by whom it was made, as well as what he thinks it might fetch at auction.

Should you decide to sell, the valuer should also advise you whether a "reserve" price is necessary. A reserve is the minimum price for which the auctioneer may sell your property, and can act as an important safeguard if the sale turns out to be very poorly attended. You should also remember to ask the valuer how quickly your property will be sold. If the property is of exceptional quality you may be advised to wait for a particular sale which will feature other good quality objects and attract better prices. Certain specialist sales are only held once or twice a year, and it may be that you could sell more quickly elsewhere.

THE COST OF SELLING

An auction house does not buy your property from you, instead it sells on your behalf. For this service you will be charged a commission and costs, such as insurance and illustration (when necessary).

An auction house expert giving an over-the-counter valuation.

ANTIQUES SHOPS

Antiques shops are among the easiest of places in which to begin learning about and buying antiques. They are less frantic than auction rooms, you can buy when you feel like it, and you don't have to compete with anyone else for the object of your choice.

There is an enormous variety of antiques shops, from smart West End galleries to small country dealers. Obviously your choice will be determined to some extent by personal taste and how much money you have to spend. But as in any trade there are disreputable dealers as well as honest ones, and if you are an inexperienced buyer it is very important to pick a dealer who is both knowledgeable and trustworthy.

One of the best ways to find a reputable dealer is through trade associations like the BADA and LAPADA (see p165). You can phone these organizations and ask for lists of local member dealers to be sent to you, free of charge. If, on the other hand, you are wandering down your High Street and about to enter a tantalizing shop, remember to look in the window or on the door first; a trade association sign is a good indication that the dealer has stock of good quality and also knows his subject.

Dealers who are members of organizations such as the BADA or LAPADA (or NAADAAI in America) have to undergo a rigorous selection procedure, which assesses both their stock and knowledge. Once members they are bound to keep to a strict code of practice which offers you, the buyer, reassuring protection, especially if you are about to buy something costly for the first time. Member dealers are bound to tell you as much about the piece as they can; and this includes pointing out any restoration the piece may have had. If after buying something from a member dealer, you discover it is not genuine, the organization will themselves organize a panel of independent experts to investigate your claim and make sure, if it is upheld, you get a full and speedy refund. Remember that even the best-intentioned dealers can make the odd genuine mistake. But a good dealer will want you to come back so it's not in their interests to "do" you.

The ideal antique shop should not only be reputable, it should also have a welcoming atmosphere in which you do not feel intimidated or pressurized to buy. It is worth returning to a dealer you trust because as you build up a rapport with him he will probably be able to help you in a variety of

> **BUYING FROM ANTIQUES SHOPS**
> - GET A DETAILED RECEIPT
> - DON'T RUSH, TAKE YOUR TIME
> - PICK A REPUTABLE DEALER
>
>
> LAPADA

Below The Lanes, Brighton, Sussex.
Right A general antiques shop, Brighton.

similar pieces at other shops or auction houses, to make sure the price is a fair one. It is almost expected to ask the dealer whether the price he first mentions is his "best" one. Don't feel embarrassed to do this, most are quite happy to haggle and will come down a little – one well-known London dealer even takes buyers to task if they **don't** ask for a discount!

Before you make your final decision, ask the dealer as many questions as possible about the piece. Find out how old it is, whether it's marked, what it's made from, who made it, where, and whether it has been restored.

If you decide to buy the piece, make sure you are given a full written receipt, which states the dealer's name, address and telephone number, together with the date the piece was made, a full description of it, the price you have paid, and the date of the purchase. It is very important to keep this receipt in a safe place. You will need it for insurance or in the unlikely event that the piece turns out not to be genuine.

other ways. He might let you take things home "on approval". He may operate a "buy back" scheme, which means he will let you sell back to him the objects you bought from him for the price you paid for them (a useful way of upgrading your collection). He may also look out for special things to add to your collection, and give advice and condition reports on objects you have seen at auction. Above all, a friendly dealer is one of the best ways of learning, from the inside, about your chosen subject and the fascinating world of antiques.

BUYING FROM ANTIQUES SHOPS

Unlike buying at auction, there is no pressure to buy at a particular moment from a dealer, and this gives you plenty of time to decide whether you really want the object.

Before buying any antique do try to price

JUNK SHOPS

Buying from a junk shop is rather different from buying from an antiques shop, here you must decide for yourself on the age, value and authenticity of a piece. Nonetheless if you have a keen eye, they can be fruitful sources of inexpensive collectables. Many junk shops buy their stock from house clearance sales and deceased properties where the entire contents were bought for a fixed sum. Thus you will probably find an enormous variety of different types of objects all for sale, usually for relatively inexpensive prices. Most of the items for sale in a junk shop will not be "antiques", but they are a good place to look for early 20th century furniture and decorative items.

SELLING TO AN ANTIQUES SHOP

Contrary to popular belief it is not always best to sell at auction. Selling to an antique shop has numerous advantages. Once you have reached an agreement with a dealer in an antique shop, you will probably be paid as soon as you hand over your property, and there will probably be no hidden deductions for commission, insurance etc. (see p28). Selling to a dealer saves waiting for the sale which may be several weeks away (and there is always a possibility that the object may be unsold) and waiting for payment after the sale (usually at least two weeks).

Before selling to a dealer, however, you do need to be sure of the value of your property. The public nature of auction sales means that objects of value should always realize their potential value, even if the auction house valuer has under-esti-

> ### SELLING TO ANTIQUES SHOPS
> - **FIND OUT WHICH SHOPS SPECIALIZE IN YOUR TYPE OF PROPERTY**
> - **TRY TO GET MORE THAN ONE OFFER BEFORE SELLING**
> - **NEVER SELL TO ANY-ONE WHO TURNS UP UNINVITED AT YOUR HOME**

mated them. In selling to a dealer you have no such safeguard; you get the price you agree, no more and no less.

Do a little research before offering your property for sale and find out which dealers specialize in the type of object you are offering. You are far more likely to be quoted a fair price for a Victorian chair if you take it to a dealer in 19th century furniture, than if you show it to an 18th century specialist.

If your property is too large or difficult to take to the dealer's shop, many are very happy to visit you in your home, although do make sure you pick a reputable one (see p16) before inviting him in.

There is an old adage about dealers with more than a little truth in it: if there were four dealers and one Chippendale chair on an island, all the dealers would make a living! Don't be surprised if you are offered a wide range of prices for your property as you do the rounds with it. A dealer's offer will, to some extent, be dependent on what he thinks he can sell it on for, and remember he has to make a profit or he would not be in business.

KNOCKERS

Never open your door to any "dealer" who calls uninvited, or who puts a note through your door telling you he pays cash for valuables and will return a day or two later. Many of these so called "knockers" are of very dubious integrity and their aim is to trick owners into selling their property for much less than its true value.

Opposite An antiques emporium, Portobello Road, London.
Below A variety of decorative 19th and 20th century ceramics for sale.

ANTIQUES FAIRS & MARKETS

Visiting antiques markets and fairs is a fairly effortless way of seeing a large number of dealers together and gives you a useful opportunity to compare their stock, and its quality and price. You can find out where and when they are held from local papers and antiques magazines. There are several different types of antiques markets and fairs:

- Large "vetted" fairs – where dealers from all over the country take stands and every exhibit is checked to make sure it is genuine.
- Fairs where the objects are not checked and anyone can take a stand.
- Permanent markets where specialist dealers congregate with shops and stalls every day, or several days a week.
- Weekly street markets where small traders sell goods from the early hours of the morning to other dealers, as well the general public.

VETTED FAIRS

At a large antiques fair you will probably have to pay an admission charge; for this you may be given a catalogue to the fair which lists the various dealers exhibiting and their specialities; if not, such catalogues will usually be available to buy. Many of the larger fairs which are held on a regular basis protect buyers by "vetting" all the exhibitors and their stock. This means that before the fair opens, a panel of experts on each subject will examine the items for sale on each stand to make sure they are authentic. At the best fairs, the vetting is an extremely rigorous procedure and even the most eminent dealers have been known to quake with anticipation at the arrival of the panel on their stand!

Most larger fairs operate a "dateline", which means that only objects made before a certain date may be exhibited at the fair.

The British International Antiques Fair at the National Exhibition Centre, Birmingham.

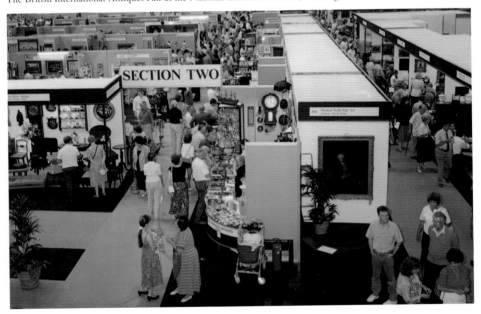

The datelines will usually be mentioned in the catalogue, but they may vary for different types of collectable. For example, pre-1900 for furniture, but pre-1930 for ceramics and pictures.

Large fairs usually feature a wide variety of different types of collectable, so you will find furniture, silver, ceramics, jewelry, textiles and much more besides, under one roof. There are also annual specialist fairs which concentrate on one particular collecting area; silver, ceramics, and even dolls all have their specialist fairs. If you are a keen collector such events can offer a golden opportunity to meet leading authorities in their field, who may come from other distant parts of the country and otherwise be difficult to visit.

If you find yourself bemused by the bustle of the fair, don't be afraid to ask for a dealer's card, and arrange to visit them at their premises after the event. All dealers see fairs as a way of meeting new collectors and forging new contacts, as well as making sales.

OTHER FAIRS

There is a world of difference between the large vetted fairs, and the plethora of smaller "antiques" fairs which are held up and down the country in church halls, schools and other similar venues. Here you may still be charged an entrance fee, but there will probably be no catalogue and no dateline or vetting, of the goods on offer. Many of the objects for sale may be better described as second-hand rather than antique, but nevertheless, provided you realize that you must satisfy yourself of the authenticity of anything you buy, such events can prove entertaining for a browse, and are sometimes a good place to buy inexpensive bric-a-brac and decorative items – and you may find a bargain.

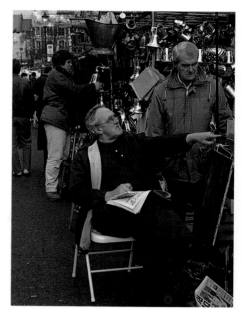

Portobello Road, London.

MARKETS

Throughout the various antiques centres in England there are many permanent antiques markets where several traders have stalls under one roof, or in a particular street (see p164). In London there are a variety of different types of market, many of which (Portobello Road for example), have become famous tourist attractions, as well as being busy antiques markets.

Highly reputable specialist dealers, many of them members of trade associations, often choose to operate from large permanent antiques markets. Visiting such markets can be a good way of discovering dealers who specialize in particularly unusual types of collectables, and the goods on offer will usually be fairly priced, because whereas a non-specialist may be inclined to over-value an object with which he is not familiar, a specialist will know precisely what it is worth and be competitive with other local traders.

Throughout the country, and especially in London, there are also weekly markets where you can buy antiques. One of the largest and most fascinating is held in Bermondsey in the East End of London from 5am every Friday morning. Here traders buy and sell to one another, as well as to

from, always get a written receipt, with the dealer's name address and a description of your purchase on it (see p16).

SELLING AT FAIRS AND MARKETS

If you have a considerable quantity of suitable goods you might want to take a stand in a local antiques fair. You can find out how to set about this from the fair organizers. If you

Bustling London market stalls at Bermondsey (above left) and Portobello Road (top and right).

private collectors, and provided you are confident enough in your particular field of interest, such markets can be wonderful sources of bargains, but you usually need to get there early to find the best buys.

BUYING FROM FAIRS AND MARKETS

Whatever type of fair or market you buy

only have a few pieces, selling direct to a market trader might be best. To sell in this way, pick a stand where they sell objects which are similar to yours, and go early, when the market is quiet. If you don't manage to sell at the first stand, avoid pickpockets by packing your treasures away carefully before you go on to the next one.

CAR BOOT SALES

Recently, a buyer at a car boot sale spotted some appealing pottery rabbits and bought them for a few pounds (see illustration on p11). The new owner then took her bunnies along to an auction house for an expert opinion. They were immediately identified as being rare early examples of Royal Doulton's *Bunnykins* series and sold soon after for nearly £4,000. Such stories are not everyday occurrences, but the mere fact that they happen at all ensures the growing appeal of the car boot sale.

Car boot sales are usually held in fields, school play grounds or car parks. They may be advertized in the classified columns of certain magazines, local papers, or simply by notices pinned up in your area. Some are regular events, held every Sunday, others are "one offs", or held only occasionally.

The boot sale is a good way of emptying the contents of your loft or garage, and raising some cash for your collection. For a small admission charge anyone can fill their car with their unwanted property and sell it for whatever they can. You can buy and sell almost anything at a boot sale – old furniture, clothes, books, electrical equipment and much more besides. If you are a collector of modest means, boot sales provide an ideal opportunity to buy relatively inexpensive collectables, but you have to be determined enough to sift through the heaps of uninteresting objects to find the tantalizing but elusive treasures.

Vintage cameras at a car boot sale.

BUYING AT A BOOT SALE

If you are about to visit a car boot sale for the first time there are a few simple guidelines which could help to make your day more successful.

Firstly, remember to arrive early. This way you will get the pick of the goods and will be more likely to spot any bargains before they are snapped up by someone else. If it's wintertime, take a torch with you; you'll need it to see what's on offer. Remember to take cash with you, preferably in coins and small notes. You can't expect people at a boot sale to welcome cheques, nor to have unlimited amounts of change available. Keep your cash in a purse belt or something similar, not only for the sake of security, but also because that leaves your hands free to examine the goodies!

If you do see something which takes your fancy, ask its price, but feel free to haggle over it. Bear in mind that there are no fixed prices at a boot sale, the objects on offer are only worth what someone is willing to pay for them.

SELLING AT A BOOT SALE

Careful planning and preparation are the key to successful selling at a boot sale. Work out what you are taking, and whether it will all fit in your car. Remember to allow space for a table, to display your property (a wall-papering table or picnic table would be ideal) and a collapsible chair to sit on. When you pack the car, try to pack the table on top, so that you don't have to unload everything on to the ground before being able to get the table out!

If you want to price things, do so clearly with sticky labels or tickets. Put on the price you would ideally like to receive, but be prepared to come down a little from this figure if need be. Remember to pack anything fragile with plenty of wrapping: newspaper and cardboard boxes are best for china and glass etc. Old blankets are useful for wrapping round pictures and prints.

Wear suitable clothes: rainwear and boots are often a good idea if the sale is in a muddy field. Take some sandwiches and a thermos of tea or coffee so you are extra well prepared for your day. Allow plenty of time for the journey, and try to arrive early so you get a good position where the maximum number of buyers will spot your goods early on, before they have spent all their money somewhere else. Don't worry if dealers rummage in your boot while you're unpacking – it can be disconcerting but it's a good way to "break the ice"! Try and take some spare change with you, (keep it safe in a purse belt) and avoid cheques whenever possible.

Finally, before the sale is over, try and arrange for a friend to come and help you. That will give you a chance to look at everyone else's offerings, and maybe spend some of your earnings at the same time.

Bargain-hunting at a boot sale.

BUYING & SELLING FROM ADVERTS

Private advertisements are an alternative way of buying and selling antiques. You may find advertisements for antiques in a wide variety of publications, from national newspapers, to specialist magazines.

One of the main worries with buying and selling through adverts is the danger to your personal safety, and the security of your property. However, provided you take the necessary precautions to minimize risks, this can be an effective way of buying and selling antiques.

BUYING FROM ADVERTS

If you're responding to an advertisement in a newspaper or magazine, try and find out as much about the piece as possible before you go and see it. Ask how big it is, what sort of condition it is in and the price.

If after all this you are still interested in the piece, make an appointment to go and see it. Find out the vendor's name as well as his address, and his home phone number if this is not the one in the advertisement. Try to go with someone else; if you must go alone, tell someone where you are going, including the name, address and phone number of the person, and when you expect to be back. When you see the piece, remember to examine it very thoroughly and make up your own mind as to its age and authenticity. If you decide to buy it, or if you have to leave a deposit, remember to ask for a written receipt, which includes the name and address of the person you are buying from and the date.

SELLING THROUGH ADVERTS

Adverts can be a good way of selling your property if you don't want to sell through a dealer or at auction, but first you must decide where to place your advert and how much your property is worth.

Your choice of publication will be dictated by both your budget and the value and type of your property. Look for a publication which has a large number of objects of a similar sort to yours. If the object you are selling might be of interest to a particular type of collector, look at the specialist collectors' magazines, as these are usually relatively inexpensive to advertize in and will reach a wider audience of potential buyers than a more general publication. If, for example you are selling an old doll, you might well be more successful by advertising in a doll collector's magazine, than in your local paper. When you have narrowed the field down, you could try phoning the numbers in one or two similar advertisements to see what sort of a response they have had.

Before you place the advertisement, find out what your property is worth. Show the object to a few reputable dealers, or take it to an auction house to get a good idea of what you could reasonably ask for it.

Word the advertisement clearly and succinctly, try to mention the age of the piece if you know it. You can either give a box number or your phone number for interested buyers to respond to, but don't mention your name and address because this might encourage burglars.

If you have left a telephone number, try to be in to take calls when the publication first appears, and be prepared to give callers a full detailed description over the phone. It is quite a good idea to take a deposit from anyone who says they want to buy the object but will come back at a later date to pay and collect it. That way you will ensure you do get paid and will not lose out on other potential buyers who may respond to your advertisement. Try to avoid cheques; cash or a banker's order are much safer.

PART 2

BRINGING
IT HOME

ABOVE UNWRAPPING A 19TH CENTURY CARRIAGE
CLOCK.

LEFT PORCELAIN DISPLAYED IN PURPOSE-BUILT
CABINETS.

VALUING & INSURING

No keen collector enjoys contemplating the thought of losing a prized possession, but unfortunately, an unpleasant aspect of collecting antiques today is the growing risk of burglary. One result of the increasing number of art and antiques thefts is that most insurance companies now demand a professional written valuation to cover objects worth more than a certain amount.

If you are beginning to buy antiques you will certainly know what each piece is worth, and whether you need a valuation. But supposing you bought them a decade or more ago, or have been given or inherited them, do you really know what they're worth, and for what sum they should be insured? In recent years, many types of antiques have risen dramatically in value. Numerous, once modestly-valued objects are now worth substantial sums, so if you're unsure as to the value of your collection, and whether you need a valuation, it's a good idea to take professional advice. Remember, although a valuation will involve some expense, if you don't have your possessions valued you could find that in the event of burglary or accident, you are inadequately insured and unable to replace your property.

VALUATIONS

There are various ways of having your antiques valued. If you know a friendly local dealer, and only have a few items, he may be able to provide you with a valuation, although you should check with your insurance company that this will be acceptable. If you have a fairly extensive collection, your insurance company may prefer a valuation from a specialist valuer, or one of the larger auction houses, all of whom have large valuations departments.

One of the main advantages in using an auction house is that although most of the valuing will be done by "generalists" (valuers with experience in assessing many different types of antiques) if there is anything unusual in your collection, or anything they are unsure of, they can call upon specialist experts for advice. Every year an

Opposite A Japanese *cloisonné* vase c.1910, discovered by one of Bonham's insurance valuers. Its owner thought it was worth around £2,000. The vase was identified as the work of one of Japan's most prominent *cloisonné* craftsmen, Kyoto Namikawa, and later sold for over £60,000.

Below Valuation documents are required by increasing numbers of insurance companies.

amazing number of valuable treasures come to light when auction house valuers visit collectors' homes. Among the most extraordinary finds of recent years, are a priceless Ming bowl being used for a dog's water, and a medieval bronze employed as a door stop! Both of these were later sold for several thousand pounds.

THE COST OF VALUING

Before you decide on who to call in to value your property, do shop around and look for the best deal. Prices for valuations vary, and can be calculated in various ways, either as a percentage of the total value of your property (usually between ½% and 1½%), on a daily rate, or as an agreed flat rate. As a general guide, a valuer will be able to assess between 100-300 pieces per day. To some extent the fee you are quoted for your valuation will depend upon how much the auction house wishes to secure you as a client. To an auction house, a valuation is recognized as being an important way of establishing loyalty with their firm. So the chances are that if you have an unusually extensive collection say, of Dinkies, the auction house will be keen to lure you to their firm, and may be prepared to negotiate. You should always make sure you agree the final figure before the valuation takes place, not afterwards. Some auction houses offer an added bonus by reducing their commission rates, should you decide to sell any of the items they have valued within a reasonably short period of time.

Whoever carries out your valuation, you should make sure it includes a full description of every item, together with its dimensions and value for insurance purposes. The value placed upon each object will to some extent depend on where you would go to replace your property; would you go shopping in Bond Street, or at your local auction house? The price an insurance valuer puts on your property will probably be at least 20% higher than what you could expect to get should you decide to sell. If you feel this will make your insurance premiums prohibitively high, you can opt for "market valuations" — in other words auction prices — instead. But bear in mind if the valuation is too low you could find yourself unable to replace lost items satisfactorily.

INSURING

The person you choose to value your antiques may be able to advise you on a suitable insurer. One way of reducing premiums is to shop around. If your collection is moderately large and valuable you will probably find it is less expensive to insure through a broker specializing in art and antiques, rather than through a large composite insurer. Whereas a large insurer will usually lump together your antiques in the general household policy, a specialist broker will assess the risk of different categories of antique individually, therefore reducing premiums. Usually furniture and large items are less expensive to insure than small, easily portable items.

SECURITY

There are two important ways in which you can protect your collection. Firstly, you should try to deter potential thieves from entering your home by making it as secure as possible. If you are unsure about how to go about this, you can contact the crime prevention officer through your local police station. He will advise you on safeguarding your belongings and can also recommend reputable security firms in your area to install additional locks or alarms or whatever other equipment may be necessary.

But what if disaster should strike, and you do find yourself the victim of crime? You can assist the recovery of your property by marking your belongings with a security pen (available through the Crime Prevention officer) which only shows up under an ultraviolet light. However, many collectors prefer not to mark their antiques in this way, because the pen is indelible, and should you want to sell the item at a later date it could deter prospective buyers. By far the best way of helping the police to retrieve your possessions is by supplying them with as much information about your stolen property as possible. An inventory, or list of your collection, will be invaluable for this (see p31 Documenting), but it is also vitally important to have a clear photograph of each object in your collection.

Photographs of any stolen antiques can be logged via your local police officer with the Art and Antiques Squad at Scotland Yard. This police department has a national data-base, which contains descriptions and photographic images of works of art stolen throughout the country. When stolen property is recovered, the Art and Antiques squad can identify the rightful owner – provided the object has been logged on their computer system. But you do need a photograph to stand a good chance of success. It's salutary to remember that the vast majority of stolen antiques the police recover are never claimed. In such cases not only does the culprit evade prosecution, but the property is returned to him! Photographing your property, you will help to redress this balance, and increase your chances of recovering stolen items.

THE ART AND ANTIQUES POLICE SQUAD'S TIPS

- PHOTOGRAPH AGAINST A PLAIN BACKGROUND – WHITE OR GREY IS USUALLY BEST
- TRY AND FILL THE VIEW FINDER WITH THE IMAGE
- PUT A RULER BESIDE EACH OBJECT TO GIVE AN IDEA OF SCALE
- PHOTOGRAPH MARKS, CHIPS, DENTS, SCRATCHES

PHOTOGRAPHING

You may want to enlist the help of a professional photographer to photograph your collection, although, if you observe a few simple guidelines it is quite a simple task to do it yourself. It is best to photograph objects using colour film outdoors in natural daylight. Choose a day when there's a light cloud cover, so the sunlight is not too harsh and the shadows aren't very noticeable. For the clearest results, you can use either standard 35mm 100 ASA print film or the new, specially improved Polaroid camera. The older type of Polaroids, although frequently used for the purposes of research by auction houses, are not generally very satisfactory long term photographic records, as the colours can be unstable and fade. The new Polaroid cameras are available on free loan from the Crime Prevention Officers of many police stations, but you have to supply your own film.

To get the best results stand with the sun behind you, level with the object, not above or to the side, and close enough to fill the view finder. If the objects are very small, photograph them against a plain background; white is usually the best colour for this, unless the object itself is predominantly white, in which case use a grey or black background. It's also useful when photographing your collection to include a scale reference; a ruler placed beside each object is a good way of doing this. If the object is behind glass, stand slightly to one side to avoid reflections and glare.

Take at least one shot of each object, as well as close-up shots of any identifying scratches, bumps or marks on each piece. These detail shots are especially important if the object is likely to be similar to many others. If you can show the crack on the ear of your Staffordshire dog, the hallmarks of your Victorian candlestick, or the chip on the face of your carriage clock, this will provide an invaluable method of positive identification. As well as these individual photographs, it's also a good idea to take general shots of your room. These will help you to remember any smaller items which you may forget to list.

Remember to keep your photographs together in a safe place. Ideally they should be filed with your inventory entry for each object (see below). It's also a wise precaution to store a copy of photographs somewhere else for safekeeping; your bank or with your Solicitor would be ideal.

DOCUMENTING

Documenting your collection means keeping a record of every collectable object as you acquire it. It's a good idea to keep your records of each item in your collection all together in an inventory book. Then as your collection grows you will find you have a useful source of reference as well as an interesting reminder of how your collection began.

Keeping a detailed record of each object in your collection is also an ideal way to show proof of ownership in the event of an insurance claim. So any new purchase should be documented, and photographed as soon as possible after you have brought it home.

To begin your inventory of your collection make a list of every object you wish to include. Then for each object write down the following information:

● Where it came from.
● The date you bought or acquired it.
● The price you paid for it.
● A full description of the piece, including its size, what it is made from, and any decorative features.
● A report of its condition, including cracks, chips, alterations or restoration. This should be updated whenever you have the piece restored.
● Anything else you know about the object's history.

Keep the receipts of anything you have purchased with the inventory.

A detailed inventory of your collection is invaluable when claiming against burglary or damage.

DISPLAY

Antiques can be displayed in a multitude of different ways, but it's important that the method you select should be appropriate to your lifestyle. You may long to display your collection of antiques throughout your home, but if, for example, you have pets, or small children, fragile, or potentially hazardous objects should be kept well out of harm's way – perhaps on a shelf or in a cabinet out of reach. Bear in mind that not only can children or pets damage vulnerable and valuable objects, but antiques can also pose a threat to their safety. Even something as seemingly innocuous as an old teddy bear may contain wires that could harm a small child.

However, so long as you take simple precautions, there's no need to feel frightened of your collection. Many types of antiques, such as furniture, glass and silver, can still be used for their original purpose, or adapted for modern day living. Successful display should allow you to enjoy your collection as much as possible, whilst still conserving it in good condition.

Before you decide where to position your antiques, you should bear in mind how the piece was originally intended to be seen and used. Some pieces of furniture, for instance, were made to be placed against a wall, others were meant to be centrally positioned. Try and display the piece in an appropriate manner. If you have a smaller object, say a sculpture, which is meant to be seen in the round, and you have nowhere suitable to put it, you could place it in front of a mirror, so it can still be appreciated from every angle.

You may find you need to have shelves or cupboards specially constructed to house your collection. However, before you decide where to install special fittings, don't forget that nearly all types of antiques, with the exception of ceramics, silver and metalware, should be displayed away from direct sunlight and direct sources of heat (see p34). So don't, for instance, display your samplers in front of a sunny window; and keep antique furniture away from radiators. If your room is a particularly sunny one, objects such as textiles and prints can be displayed behind non-reflective, light-resistant glass, which will allow you to enjoy them whilst protecting them from fading. If you need to mount old photographs, or printed ephemera, in order to display them behind glass, use mounting tape rather than glue which can irreversibly damage the objects themselves.

If you have a collection of vases or plates, or glass, you may consider having a series of small brackets built to display them. Make sure, however, that they all sit securely on their perches. If you are displaying plates on brackets, they will need to be propped up on plate stands. Before climbing up to put them in their final resting place, it's a good idea to test them on their stands at an accessible height, so you can check they are firm and unlikely to roll off. Plates and ceramic flatwares can also be simply hung on a wall by using a wire and spring plate rack. These come in a wide variety of sizes, so make sure you choose the right one, as if it's too small and it could put the plate under strain and cause it to crack, and if it's too large the plate could fall down. To check the size is right put the hanger on top of the rack, it should be about 2cms/1 inch smaller than the diameter of the plate before you stretch it.

Shelves are also an effective way of displaying a wide variety of antiques. If you are planning to put several heavy objects on a shelf, make sure it's suitably strong, take advice from your builder if necessary. Don't forget that objects which are openly displayed will need periodic dusting, so it's no good putting them somewhere where it will be impossible for you to reach them from time to time. If you don't want to have to dust so often, consider putting your collection in a glass cabinet or display case.

Small antiques are often more effectively displayed together, rather than dotted around a room. If you have a collection of small silver objects or boxes it might be a good idea to display them on an attractive tray, a dish, or even on a small table.

Antiques of different types look very attractive when displayed together, but always be careful before standing objects directly on top of old furniture. Silver and metal objects, particularly pieces with feet, can scratch the surface of furniture, so if in doubt place them on a mat to protect the wood.

Among the many aids to the effective display of collections of antiques are pedestals, stands and hangers. Most of these can be purchased through department and good hardware stores. Other specialized pieces of display equipment are available by mail order through specialist magazines.

Finally, once you've displayed your col-

Opposite Blue and white vases displayed on brackets.
Above A collection of porcelain displayed in an alcove.

lection, don't forget the importance of lighting it effectively, but bear in mind that if you place objects too close to powerful lighting they may be damaged by the heat. Nevertheless, a carefully positioned spotlight on your display will invariably create a dramatic focal point in any room, whether it's a cluster of plates on a cottage wall, or a group of priceless porcelain on the mantelpiece of a mansion!

CARE & RESTORATION

Looking after your antiques correctly is essential if they are to remain in good enough condition for future generations to enjoy as much as you do. Nevertheless, there is a world of difference between correctly caring for an antique and attempting to restore it to mint condition. Nearly all antiques reflect their age and you shouldn't expect them to look too perfect.

In general, restoration reduces value; a piece with limited wear and tear will nearly always be preferable and more valuable than one which has been over-restored. Nonetheless, if your antique is in danger of deteriorating further because of the damage it has sustained, or if its imperfections are impairing your use and enjoyment of it, it may benefit from limited restoration. If this is the case, always consult a specialist restorer. Unskilled restoration can cause irreversible damage to an antique and may greatly reduce value.

Nearly all antiques, apart from silver, ceramics and glass, should be protected from direct sunlight and heat. Sunlight causes textiles, carpets, prints and furniture to fade. Direct sources of heat cause many substances, including wood and *papier mâché* to expand. This may lead to warping and splitting in antique furniture, and can cause cracking or flaking in pieces made from a *papier mâché* core with a painted surface.

Prolonged exposure to cigarette, pipe and tobacco smoke can cause discoloration in many types of antiques which can be tricky to restore. So always keep antiques in a well ventilated room, and protect them from excessive smoke.

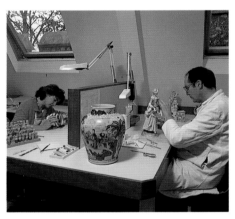

Porcelain restoration at West Dean College, Sussex.

Some general guidelines for caring for the main categories of antiques are listed below, other tips on caring for specific types of collectables are contained in Part 3.

FURNITURE
● Excessively dry conditions can cause veneers to lift, and joints to dry out. If your home is very well heated it may be worth investing in a humidifier to protect your furniture. Excessively damp conditions are also detrimental to furniture as the wood may rot.

● If pieces of veneer break off don't throw them away; keep them safely as it's always preferable to use original veneers and they will reduce the cost of restoration.

● Avoid silicone polishes and aerosol sprays; instead use a small amount of good quality wax polish from a tin or jar. Don't over-polish or the piece will become sticky.

● Never drag furniture when you want to move it as this causes strain on the legs – pick it up instead. Don't risk picking a piece up by its carrying handles (these are usually more decorative than functional), or by the top if it has a protruding rim; always support the main structure.

CERAMICS AND GLASS

When ceramic pieces are cracked or damaged, the current trend is to leave damage showing, rather than attempt to disguise it completely. Cracked pieces may be stuck together with a suitable glue, but they should not be overpainted. Chips may be filled and coloured to match, but should not be overpainted.

- Pottery, porcelain and glass can be cleaned occasionally, by hand, with warm soapy water and should be rinsed well before drying. Decanters should be stored with their stoppers off.

Restoration department at Sotheby's, London.

- Don't secure loose lids or stoppers with adhesive tape or adhesive paste as these can damage original gilding and enamel.

SILVER

Contrary to popular opinion, silver doesn't tarnish especially rapidly unless it's kept in a particularly damp atmosphere. Any proprietary silver polish may be used and a toothbrush may be handy to remove polish from nooks and crannies. Always make sure that you remove all traces of polish, or it can clog up decorated areas. Don't overpolish silver, or you may erase decoration, and, eventually, wear the metal thin. You can wash silver, by hand, in warm soapy water. Don't put it in the dishwasher as the abrasive powder dulls the surface. Silver gilt doesn't need cleaning with polish; an occasional wash with soapy water should be enough.

- Don't over-polish Sheffield and electroplate items as you will wear away the thin surface layer of silver.
- Never leave salt in cruets or cellars; salt may get under the glass liner and can cause corrosion spots.

CLOCKS

Most maintenance should be left to a specialist, although wooden cases can be carefully dusted and waxed occasionally. Brass and silvered dials are protected by lacquer and should never be polished or placed in contact with water or detergent.

- Cleaning and oiling the clock's movement should be carried out with great care by a specialist.
- Clocks with spring-drive and short pendulums can be carried from one room to another, but should be held upright. For long distance journeys the pendulum must be secured or removed. Longcase clocks should be dismantled before being moved.

CARPETS, RUGS AND TEXTILES

Carpets and rugs should be cleaned by brushing or beating (so long as they are not very frail).

- Placing underlay beneath an antique carpet will absorb wear and protect the pile.
- Sunlight can cause colours to fade and fibres to rot. Framed textiles can be protected behind special light-resistant glass.
- Unless they are very fragile, most textiles can be washed with warm soapy water.

PART 3

COLLECTOR'S
COMPENDIUM

ABOVE MEISSEN BLUE AND WHITE SHAPED
RECTANGULAR DISH, £4,140.

LEFT DOLLS AND TEDDY BEARS ON
DISPLAY IN AN ANTIQUES SHOP.

Of all the categories of antiques you can choose to collect, furniture is among the most popular and practical. Many pieces offer you the alternative of using them either for their original purpose, or of adapting them to modern day living. Furniture differs from other types of antiques in that you probably don't want to collect it by the type of object – nobody wants a room full of only chests or tables – but you may have an affinity for a particular wood, or style of decoration. Whatever your preference, you need to familiarize yourself with the styles, methods of construction, and types of material used, in order to determine whether the piece is "right" (in other words, in its original condition without any major alterations or additions) or "wrong" (some major change has been made to it, or it's a fake).

The following pages discuss some of the most common types of furniture you'll come across, and give you hints about what to look out for. Once you've read them, visit as many auctions and dealers as possible before you begin to buy. Don't be afraid to pull out drawers, get down on the floor and look under table tops, and lift up chairs to look at their legs. Remember there's no better way of learning about the subject than by hands-on experience!

BASICS

No matter what type of furniture you're interested in, there are certain basic features which you need to take into account before you decide whether the piece is genuine, when it was made, and how much it might be worth. Identifying the wood used, the type of construction, the decoration and quality of workmanship are all crucial in helping you to make up your mind. These fundamental points, which apply to many different types of furniture, are discussed on the following four pages.

WOODS

At first furniture was made from solid wood, but as cabinet-making improved, the technique of decorating furniture by applying veneers (thin sheets of wood) developed. This was an economical way of using expensive woods, and allowed the maker to create decorative effects from the different grains and patterns (called figuring) of the wood. Veneered furniture has a carcass (solid body) made from a different (usually less expensive) wood. This secondary wood, as it is known, is most commonly pine or oak. Listed below are examples of the most frequently seen types of woods used for antique furniture.

AMBOYNA

Richly coloured wood with a tight grain, used during the 18th century and Regency periods, nearly always as a veneer.

BEECH

Brownish-whitish wood used in the solid from the 17th century for the frames of upholstered furniture, because it doesn't split when tacked. Also popular during the 18th and 19th centuries as base for painted furniture.

CHERRY

Orange-brown wood popular for American Queen Anne and Chippendale furniture. Usually used in the solid.

CHESTNUT

Ranges in tone from light to dark brown,

much used during the 18th century for French provincial furniture made in the solid.

COROMANDEL
A dark boldly figured wood, almost black in parts with pale striations, used mainly as a veneer for refined furniture of the Regency period.

EBONY
Dense, heavy, almost black wood, often used as a contrasting inlay in marquetry veneering.

ELM
Light brown coloured wood, popular for Windsor chairs and provincial English furniture.

MAHOGANY

Rich golden-brown or red-brown coloured wood, became popular in England from c.1730. There are several types of mahogany, San Domingan, Cuban, Honduras and Spanish are most common.

OAK

Deep rich chocolate-brown, or paler golden-brown coloured coarse-grained wood used predominantly in Britain from Middle Ages to late 17th century. Also used as a secondary wood on good quality furniture.

PINE
Soft pale honey coloured wood used in England and America as a secondary timber for drawer linings, and in the 19th century for inexpensive furniture (which was often painted).

ROSEWOOD

Highly figured dark red-brown wood with blackish streaks. Popular during the Regency and Victorian periods in England for high quality furniture.

SATINWOOD

Light yellow-coloured West Indian wood, favoured during the late 18th century. Usually used in veneers as it was expensive, and sometimes embellished with painted decoration. Painted satinwood furniture was also popular in the Edwardian period.

VIRGINIA WALNUT
Richly coloured wood resembling mahogany. Used in the solid and as a veneer on English and American furniture from c.1730.

WALNUT

Nutty or honey brown highly figured wood used in the solid on English furniture from c.1660–c.1690 and as veneers from c.1690–c.1735. Walnut was also popular in America and in the Victorian era.

YEW
Red-brown hardwood used both in veneers or in the solid on the best English provincial furniture of the 17th and 18th centuries.

COLOUR AND PATINA
A rich mellow colour is one of the most important features of any piece of furniture. The **patina** is the glow the wood develops over the years from an accumulation of wax polish and dirt.
- Most furniture is not the same colour all over – grooves and carving will look darker, surfaces exposed to sunlight may be lighter.

PROPORTIONS
The proportions are fundamental in assessing the quality of a piece, and deciding whether it's "right".
- A piece which looks too heavy on top, or has legs which are too big or small may well be a "marriage" (see p41).
- Small pieces are usually more desirable.

CONSTRUCTION

Early furniture was made using mortice-and-tenon joints held by pegs or dowels (below) instead of glue or screws. This

method was used until the late 17th century. Pegs were hand-made and stand slightly proud of the surface.

● Later machine-made pegs are perfectly symmetrical,

and are either flush with the surface or slightly recessed.
● From the early 18th century joints were dovetailed and glued (above).

● Until the end of the 18th century, when the circular saw was introduced, all wood was sawed by hand and has straight saw marks. After c.1800 circular marks may be visible on the surface of unfinished wood.

SCREWS

The earlier the screw the cruder it will be.
● The groove on old screws tends to be off-centre and the top irregular (above).
● The thread is also irregular and open and, unlike modern screws (below), runs the entire length of the shank.

DRAWERS

● Dovetails are the triangular joints which slot together on the corners of drawers. They became progressively finer (see p43) and can help with dating.
● Drawers had channels in their sides and, until the 18th century, ran

on runners set into the carcass.
● Some drawers ran on the dust boards and had no runners.
● From the Queen Anne period the runners were placed under the drawer at the sides and ran on bearers placed on the inside of the carcass.

HANDLES

● Handles can provide a useful clue to dating, because styles changed from period to period (see p42).
● It's common to find pieces with replaced handles; this isn't serious but it's preferable to have handles in keeping with the rest of the piece.
● From c.1690 handles were secured by pommels and nuts.

● Antique pommels were hand-cast in a single piece of brass (above). The thread goes only halfway up the shank, and

the remainder of the shank is square-shaped. Modern pommels (below) are made from brass heads with steel shanks and the thread runs the whole length of the shank.
● The nuts used to attach handles in the 18th century were circular and slightly irregular. Modern nuts are regular and hexagonal.

FEET

Feet can give a useful guide to dating (see p42); however, centuries of standing on damp floors often causes feet to rot and many have been replaced.
● Compare the wood of the feet with that of the rest of the body to decide whether or not they're original.

LOCKS

● Early locks are usually of wrought iron held in place with iron nails. From the 18th century locks were steel or brass and secured with steel screws.
● Locks are often replaced; this isn't

serious although it's better to have original ones.

CARVING

Oak was relatively difficult to carve but as walnut and mahogany became popular carving became finer and more intricate.

- Original carved decoration adds to the desirability of a piece.
- Some pieces were adorned with later carving; these are far less desirable than those with original decoration.

VENEERING

The quality of veneering has an important bearing on price.

- Many pieces have *quarter-veneered* tops, where four pieces of wood create a pattern.
- *Banding*, strips of veneers laid around the edges of drawers, were also popular. Depending on the way in which the grain of the wood runs, banding is referred to as *straight banding, cross banding, feather* or *herring bone banding*.

INLAY/ MARQUETRY

A pattern made from veneers of differently coloured woods (see p44). Inlaying was popular on English and Continental furniture from the 17th century and can add greatly to the value of a piece.

CONDITION

Furniture in original pristine condition commands the highest prices and is always scarce.

- Don't dismiss pieces with blemishes – so long as the wood itself has not been damaged; surface spots can often be treated by a good restorer. The table (above) may look rather scruffy but the wood itself is undamaged and could easily be repolished.

WOODWORM

Small round holes in old furniture are a common sight in old furniture and show that the piece has at some stage been attacked by woodworm.

- These need not put you off, provided the infestation hasn't structurally weakened the piece.
- Active woodworm can be detected by pale coloured powder in the worm holes, or on adjacent surfaces, and should be treated with a proprietary product as soon as possible.
- Check periodically for signs of infestation.

MARRIAGES

A piece of furniture made up from separate items which did not originally belong together is termed a "marriage".

- The married parts may be of a similar period or one part may be later, or even modern.
- Marriages are nearly always much less desirable than pieces in original condition.
- Examine furniture

in the way described on p38 to make sure it isn't a marriage.

ALTERATIONS

Furniture which has been altered is usually less desirable than that in its original condition. Among the most common alterations are large pieces which have been reduced in size. Freshly cut surfaces, repositioned handles, and plugged holes are signs of alteration.

FAKES

A piece of furniture can be described as fake if it deliberately makes you think it's older than it really is. Fakes made from new timber are usually easy to spot as the wood doesn't have the patina of age you would expect. Some fakes are made from old wood and these can be more tricky to identify. Beware of any piece being sold as 18th century or earlier if it has circular saw marks (see p40). These mean the wood was cut after c.1800 when circular saws were first used. Specific types of fake are dealt with in Part 3.

CHESTS

Chests of drawers are among the most indispensable pieces of furniture for storage and, not surprisingly, have been made in huge numbers over the centuries. They are still among the most easily available and inexpensive pieces of antique furniture – although of course there are rare and expensive ones as well.

A chest has many of the elements found in other types of furniture – drawers, feet, handles and so on – and if you're keen to learn how to date and authenticate any type of antique furniture, examining a chest carefully can teach you a great deal.

STYLES OF FEET
Feet can give a useful clue to the date.

Stile foot
17thC

Early bracket foot
late 17thC

Ogee bracket foot
1750–1800

Bun foot
17th–early 18thC

Bracket foot
18thC

Splayed
bracket foot
late 18thC–
early 19thC

HANDLE STYLES

Late 17th
–early
18thC

Early
18thC

2nd quarter 18thC

2nd half
18thC

Late 18thC
–early
19thC

◀ **WALNUT CHESTS**
Size has an important bearing on the price of all chests. Although this walnut veneered 18th century chest is in a sorry state, it's desirably small (77cm/2ft 6in wide) and so is still worth £1,500-3,500.

▼ **MAHOGANY CHESTS**
Mahogany chests, such as this (made c.1765), are more common than walnut ones and so are usually less expensive. This chest is of exceptionally high quality, but even so need not cost much more than the battered walnut one above. £2,000-3,500.

WHY DO DEALERS LOOK IN DRAWERS?

Pull the drawer out and look for marks on the dustboards inside the chest – if the chest is original the marks of the runners should correspond with marks on the bottom of the drawer. From c.1790 drawers were strengthened by baseboards running from side to side with a central rib.

CONSTRUCTION

Examine the dovetails – they can tell you when the drawer was made. The earliest drawers have three coarse dovetails; later drawers usually have four or five finer ones. Don't just look at one drawer – check they're all similar.

THIS MAHOGANY CHEST WAS MADE *c.*1790. THE BOW-FRONTED STYLE REMAINED POPULAR THROUGHOUT MUCH OF THE 19TH CENTURY. £450-3,000

HANDLES

Check drawers inside and out for marks, such as holes or an outline of a handle shape, where different handles might once have been. Don't be put off if the handles are replaced – it's very common.

UNDERSIDES

Don't expect chests to be neatly finished all the way round. They were made to stand against a wall and their backs and undersides are usually made from rough unpolished boards.

FEET

The feet are most prone to wear and are often replaced, so check the colour and grain of each one. These feet are original and appropriately battered.

DRESSERS, CABINETS & CREDENZAS

In most collectors' minds antique dressers epitomise "country" style and rustic charm. They give instant atmosphere to a room and can look equally impressive in a dining room, kitchen or hall – or wherever else you care to put them. According to the style you are looking for, dressers vary greatly in price; those made from simple pine in the 19th century, or later, are most affordable; early oak ones are usually very much more expensive.

Cabinets are among the most refined – and valuable – pieces of antique furniture available. They were made in the 17th and 18th centuries to store precious curiosities, and became status symbols reflecting the wealth of their owner. Cabinets can create a dramatic focal point in a room – but unless you are extremely lucky, you may have to dig deep in your pockets to be able to afford an early one.

If you seek a more affordable elegance look out for 19th century credenzas. Like cabinets, credenzas were made to display valuables, and are often highly ornate and decorative. Unlike most early cabinets, however, many are still available relatively inexpensively.

▼ CABINETS
Legs on cabinets have often been replaced. Even though the stand of this *c.*1690 oyster laburnum marquetry cabinet is a later replacement (it has a harsh glossy finish quite different from the mellow sheen of the rest of the piece), the cabinet is still very valuable and worth around £9,000.

MARQUETRY

Marquetry

Oyster veneer

Stringing

Cross banding

Secondary wood

Marquetry decoration, as on the cabinet above, **always** adds to value. Terms used to describe the different techniques are:

● **Oyster veneering:** slices cut across branches to make patterns like an oyster shell.

● **Cross banding:** border with a grain at right angles to the main veneer.

● **Parquetry:** geometric pattern of small pieces of veneer.

● **Stringing:** narrow line of inlaid wood.

WHAT TO LOOK FOR

Early (pre-*c*.1800) Dressers
- simple joined construction
- rather crudely made drawers
- at least three drawers across base – if there are two it may have been reduced in size.

DRESSERS

Beware of dressers where the base and rack have been "married" and did not originally belong together.

Compare the colour and patina of the wood on both parts – here the colour of rack and base are similar, showing that they belong together.

Look for the outline of the rack on the base, such as you can see here. £3,000-5,000
REMEMBER – not all dressers had racks.

▶ CREDENZAS

Credenzas can still be bought for under £1,000 – a bargain considering their usual good quality, especially when you compare them with the cost of earlier similarly elaborate pieces. This one is worth around £750-950 and has many desirable features:
- walnut veneers
- original glass
- gilt mounts
- attractive inlay.

CHAIRS

Chairs are among the most essential pieces of furniture, and not surprisingly the finest antique ones – usually those made in the l8th century or earlier – can be very valuable. Prices for dining chairs are not only affected by quality and age but also by the number of chairs in the set – the longer the set the more expensive each chair becomes. But if you choose a simple pattern you may be able to find odd numbers of chairs and build up a set piecemeal.

The first chairs were simply constructed like stools, with a plank of wood at the back which sometimes had carved decoration. During the second half of the 17th century walnut replaced oak as the favourite wood and chairs were often elaborately carved with scrolls on stretchers and legs.

Mahogany chairs became popular during the 18th century, and chair styles reflected designs published by leading designers such as Chippendale, Hepplewhite and Sheraton. Their pattern books were circulated nationwide to cabinet-makers, who reproduced the designs, often in much simplified form. Nowadays, when a chair is described as "Chippendale", "Hepplewhite" or "Sheraton" it usually means it is based on one of their patterns rather than made by the cabinet maker himself.

DATING

18th C — leg, seat rail

corner brace all just glued

brace

19th C — leg, seat rail

corner bracket glued and screwed

corner bracket

Before the 19th century, chair seat frames were strengthened with glued corner braces. After c.1840 shaped and screwed triangular brackets were used.

▼ **EARLY OAK CHAIRS**
Carving can help identify a chair's origins. This one dates from c.1640 and is carved with the dragon crest and scrolled arms typical of the Gloucestershire region. £1,000-5,000

▲ **WALNUT CHAIRS**
This c.1720 walnut chair has the cabriole legs and drop-in seat characteristic of chairs of the period. High quality chairs of this date would not have had stretchers, so this one was probably made by a provincial maker. £300+

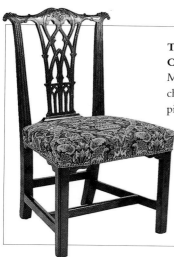

THOMAS CHIPPENDALE

Many of Chippendale's chair designs featured pierced splats carved with scrolling foliage and incorporating Gothic elements, as seen on this *c*.1765 chair. Ribbons and chinoiserie details were also popular. £750+

WHAT TO LOOK FOR

- Examine chairs carefully for signs of genuine wear and the patina of age – nearly all types have been reproduced at some time since the 19th century.
- If the colour of one part looks very different it may be a replacement.
- Thick brown varnish often indicates a chair trying to look older than it is.

▼ REGENCY CHAIRS

This *c*.1800 painted chair, with gilded decoration, slender arms and ebonized and tapered front legs is typical of the early Regency period. Later chairs were more heavily proportioned. £500–1,800

▼ BALLOON-BACKED CHAIRS

The value of this *c*.1860 Victorian walnut balloon-back chair is increased by its fine proportions and desirable needlework seat cover. £300–400

▲ WINDSOR CHAIRS

Windsors are made from country woods such as elm, oak, ash and yew and usually date from after *c*.1700. Yew Windsors, such as this one, made *c*.1810, are the most sought after. £500+

CHAIR STYLES

The changing styles of chair backs, legs and feet can help collectors to date chairs. The artworks below show a selection of the more commonly-seen designs. However, as most of these were repeated in later periods, the style of a chair must be seen only as a guide to its age, not as proof of its authenticity.

CHAIR BACKS
1. Early 16thC bobbin frame
2. Cromwellian padded
3. Late 17thC bobbin turned
4. Early 18thC Queen Anne hoop-back with urn-shape splat
5. Ladder-back with horizontal pierced splats, c.1760
6. Chippendale-style with carved splat c.1760
7. "Chinese" Chippendale chair c.1760
8. Plain mahogany Chippendale-style chair c.1760
9. Late 18thC Hepplewhite-style shield back
10. Late 18thC Gothic style chair
11. Late 18thC lyre-back
12. Early 19thC country style ladder back
13. Late 18thC hoop-back with wheatsheaf splat
14. Sheraton-style arm chair c.1790
15. Early 19thC Sheraton-style square framed
16. Late 18thC Gothic Windsor
17. Early 19thC spindle-back
18. Early 19thC plain Windsor

19. Regency with key pattern c.1820
20. Regency rope twist c.1820
21. Early Victorian c.1840
22. Gothic square-backed c.1830
23. Victorian carved balloon-back c.1850
24. Mid-19thC Victorian Carolean

LEGS AND FEET
1. 16thC baluster
2. Late 17thC bobbin turned
3. Second half 17thC barley-twist
4. Inverted cup baluster c.1675-1700
5. Late 17thC double scroll
6. Early 18thC cabriole
7. Early 18thC carved cabriole
8. 18thC shell carved cabriole
9. Early Georgian carved cabriole
10. Mid-18thC cabriole with claw-and-ball foot
11. Chamfered c.1750-80
12. Mid-18thC blind fretted
13. Late 18thC turned
14. Early 19thC sabre
15. Victorian Carolean c.1845
16. Mid-19thC reeded

UPHOLSTERED CHAIRS & SOFAS

No home would be complete without comfy sofas and chairs, and antique upholstered furniture can be less expensive than modern counterparts – and surprisingly comfortable as well.

Among the most popular types of chairs are winged armchairs with simple cabriole legs and side panels to keep out chilly draughts. These were first made in the early 18th century and the design has remained virtually unchanged to this day. The wooden frame is the most important part of antique chairs and sofas, so never buy a chair with a severely damaged frame. Don't worry too much about the condition of upholstery — as this can usually be restored.

WING ARM CHAIRS

◀ SIGNS OF AGE
The marks of the original upholstery nails are clearly visible here and are a good sign of authenticity.

▲ BEFORE
Although this arm-chair (shown on the right after re-upholstering) looks terribly tatty, being able to see it like this is a bonus – you can make sure the wood is original and hasn't split or been weakened by woodworm.
● If the chair is recently re-covered, ask if there are photos of the frame.

▶ AFTER
It's very rare to find a chair with its original covering but provided the fabric is in a style appropriate to the chair this doesn't greatly affect value – this 18th century chair is covered in a suitable silk damask. £5,000+

18TH CENTURY DROP-IN SEAT

cover

padding

webbing

horsehair stuffing · outer padding

scrim

cover

hessian

coil springs

webbing

19TH CENTURY SPRUNG UPHOLSTERY

WHAT'S INSIDE A CHAIR?

Before *c.*1830 the uphol-stery on chairs was made from thin layers of horsehair and padding supported by webbing covered with fabric. Upholstery using coiled metal springs covered with padding and webbing was made from *c.*1830.

▲ REGENCY CHAISES LONGUES
The outward curving "sabre" legs, dark painted wood, and "anthemion" flower decorations are clear signs that this elegant chaise longue dates from the Regency period (*c.*1815). Although not very comfortable, chaises longues have become enormously popular recently; this one could fetch £6,000 or more.

◀ BUTTON BACKS
Before buying a Victorian button back, turn it upside down and look for a manufacturer's mark or label; these can add greatly to value – Howard & Sons' labels are especially desirable – they made the "Rolls Royce" of chairs! This one is worth over £3,000, but you can find them from £500+.

DINING TABLES

PEDESTAL TABLES

Elegant pedestal tables are so practical and popular that they have been made continuously from the 18th century to the present day. Value depends largely on age and number of pedestals. A 19th century one such as this might cost from £3,000 upwards, a modern version £300-500.

BEFORE YOU BUY IT . . . fit any extra leaves in the table to check they aren't warped.

SIGNS OF AGE
- solid mahogany tops – usually without crossbanding or inlay
- "reeded" edge to tops
- brass casters — plain or cast as lion's paws.

There are many different types of dining table to choose from, depending on what size you require – and how much you want to spend. Remember to look at the grain of the wood on the top – an attractively grained top is a definite plus but will increase the price. If you're on a limited budget don't dismiss tables which have marked tops – so long as the wood has not been damaged it can probably be restored to its former glory. Don't forget to sit down at the table to make sure it feels a comfortable height and the legs don't get in the way of yours.

WHAT TO LOOK FOR

- Signs of wear on the legs and top – scratches and marks are a sign of genuine age and to be expected.
- Legs of more or less the same colour – if one is different it might be a replacement.
- Flaps which match the rest of the table reasonably well – those used only occasionally may not have faded as much as the rest of the table top but their figuring should be similar.

◀ REFECTORY TABLES

These are among the earliest dining tables, most date from the 17th-18th centuries, but there are also fakes around – many made from old floor boards. Look for circular saw marks – these show the table is not as old as it seems and has been made or tampered with since the 19th century. This one dates from *c*.1620 and is worth over £10,000.

▶ DROP LEAF TABLES

Drop leafs with simple pad feet like this are among the most affordable types of 18th century tables; this one would cost around £500+

▲ D-ENDED TABLES

Adaptable D-ended tables come in several sections; the ends can be used as side tables. £1,000-4,000

▶ GATELEG TABLES

Hinged "gates" pull out to hold up the flaps on these 17th/18th century tables – hence their name. The most expensive ones seat six or more. £700+

BEWARE

Some tops are "married" (see p41) to different bases: look carefully under the top – marks which could have been made by different supports should make you suspicious.

SMALLER TABLES

Most of the myriad types of small table date from the 18th century or later. Before this, side-tables were mainly general purpose and often rectangular in shape. As fashionable society became increasingly sophisticated, furniture became more varied and elegant and a wide range of small tables designed for specific purposes, such as tea-drinking, card playing or sewing, were made. Nowadays these can be just as useful for putting the telephone on as for their original function. Small tables fit easily into most modern homes so they have remained very sought after. Pairs are always especially desirable.

WHAT TO LOOK FOR

The decoration on better quality tables can add greatly to their value – the most desirable features are:

- carved decoration on legs and feet
- tops decorated with elaborate inlay made from differently coloured woods or specimen stones
- painted decoration – popular in the late 18th century and the Edwardian period
- gilt metal mounts
- lacquer or japanning (see p58).

▶ **TRIPOD TABLES**
Carving is easily damaged and can be expensive to restore. The value of this 18th century tilt-top table is reduced because the "pie crust" rim has been chipped. £2,500

▲ **CARD TABLES**
The projecting circular corners of this 18th century table are stands for candles needed to illuminate cards and chips during play. £2,000+

◀ **WORK TABLES**
Work tables, such as this one made c.1810 from ebonized wood, have drawers and a pull out bag to hold sewing materials. £2,500+

▲ **SOFA TABLES**
The best sofa tables have two end-supports connected by a stretcher, as in this example. Tables with a central pedestal base are less valuable. £1,500-1,800

▲ PAINTED SATINWOOD
You can identify Georgian painted satinwood tables — such as this pier table made c.1775 — from those of the early 20th century by:
● the paler more mellow colour of the wood
● the less colourful painted decoration. Later tables are less valuable. This one is worth about £7,000 but would cost from about £1,000 if it was 20th-century.

TABLE STYLES

Type	First made	Price and typical wood	Description
Card & Games	c.1700	£500–2,000 mahogany, walnut, satinwood	Usually rectangular or demi-lune with folding top, baize-covered inside, specifically made for cards and other games
Console	c.1720	£1,000–5,000 giltwood	Rectangular, sometimes with serpentine front and only two front legs or carved base: made to stand against a wall
Drum	c.1800	£700–5,000 mahogany	Circular with frieze containing drawers; central pedestal support
Pembroke	c.1750	£750–6,000 mahogany, satinwood	Rectangular, serpentine or oval, with curved corners, drop flaps and drawers
Quartetto	c.1790	£800–4,000 mahogany, rosewood, walnut	Set of tables which fit under each other
Sofa	c.1790	£700–5,000 mahogany, rose-wood, satinwood	Elongated rectangle with drop flaps and drawers
Tripod	c.1700	£80–3,000 mahogany	Round tilt top, tripod base usually made from solid wood

SIDEBOARDS & DINING ACCESSORIES

Once you have chosen your table and chairs, no matter what your preferred style, there's a wealth of other antique accessories available for the dining room.

Large pieces, such as serving tables and sideboards, became extremely elegant and sophisticated during the 18th century, and many are very expensive. Much more reasonable are the wealth of 19th century sideboards available; the largest are often the most affordable.

You can also find an extraordinary array of smaller dining room accessories, such as wine coolers, urns, knife boxes, cellarets, and dumb waiters. Most were made with a very specific function in mind but can nevertheless be surprisingly versatile. These days wine coolers are more often used as containers for flowers than for wine, but they are still highly collectable.

▲ URNS
You might think that these attractive urns are purely decorative, in fact they open up and some were fitted out to hold knives, others have spouts for iced drinking water. Pairs of Georgian urns are especially desirable. These ones were made c.1775 and would cost around £4,000–6,000

18TH CENTURY SIDEBOARDS
Check legs haven't been altered: turned legs on 19th century sideboards are sometimes replaced with 18th century-style tapered ones to make a piece seem older – and more valuable. £3,500–4,000

◀ CELLARETS
Most 18th century sideboards, such as this, made c.1790, have a cellaret – a deep lead-lined drawer, to hold bottles of wine for short periods before they were served.

◀ LATER
SIDEBOARDS
**◀ LATER
SIDEBOARDS**
Provided you have
the room, you can
still find larger 19th
century sideboards in
reasonable condition
for around £750; this
one dates from *c*.1815,
and would be worth
£2,000–3,000.

HOW OLD IS IT?

This Gothic
Chippendale-style side
table might look 18th
century but in fact was
made *c*.1910. One tell-
tale sign is the dull flat
sheen of the wood – an
older piece would have
a mellow glowing
patina. £1,000–3,000

CELLARET OR WINE COOLER?

Wine coolers were
used for cooling
bottles in ice before
their contents were
drunk. They rarely
have lids and may
have a plug in the
base. Lidded
containers for storing
wine, such as this, are
described as cellarets,
but the terms
overlap. £5,000

▶ Wine coolers and
cellarets can usually be
dated from their style.

c.1760

c.1790

c.1770

c.1815

DESKS & BUREAUX

There are many different types of "writing furniture", but perhaps the best known is the bureau, basically a desk with a hinged flap that folds up when not in use. Made in quantity from the 18th century, bureaux are generally oak, walnut or mahogany, some lavishly decorated with lacquer or marquetry. They were often combined with bookcases and cabinets to become bureau bookcases or bureau cabinets. Like ordinary cabinets, these were as much to display the wealth of their owner as for any practical purpose. Many have a strong architectural feel, designed to co-ordinate with the architecture of the rooms in which they stood. Other forms of writing furniture include writing tables, kneehole desks and the curiously shaped davenport.

▼ 18TH CENTURY BUREAUX

This early 18th century bureau has many typical features which you should look for:
- small size – those wider than 107cm/42in are less desirable
- attractive walnut veneers
- bun feet, although most are replacements.

Circular marks in the baseboard (below) show that a bureau originally had bun feet (even if it now has bracket feet). £2,000-5,000

LACQUER AND JAPANNING

Chinese and Japanese lacquer became popular in the 17th century, and soon English cabinet makers began to produce their own "oriental" style lacquer called Japanning. Black was the most common colour; red, as in this desk, is much rarer.

▲ KNEEHOLE DESKS

Kneehole desks are sometimes converted from chests of drawers, so check that the drawers look complete and that veneers match. Avoid a desk with drawers on one side only – it's probably a converted washstand!
- Most desks are made from walnut, mahogany, or pine; the value of this one is substantial because the wood is covered with red japanning. £10,000+

DATING
Pediments can help with dating

Double dome top
1690-1720

Broken pediment
1730-1800

American
bonnet top
1730-1760

Swan neck
pediment
1760-1810

Regency top
1800-1830

Moulded dentil
1780-1810

▼ DAVENPORTS
There are two main
types of davenport.
Early ones were quite
plain and had an
upper section which
pulled forward to
provide the writing
surface. By c.1840
many had the
desirable "piano-rise"
top (which opens like
a piano) and a
recessed case, like the
one shown here.
Expect to pay more
for good quality
woods, like the burr
walnut of this piece,
or satinwood or
rosewood. £3,500

WHAT TO LOOK FOR
Bureau bookcases/secretaire
bookcases
● Bookcases should be
slightly smaller than their
base, but made of
matching wood.
BEWARE of bases and tops
which are flush sided – they
could be a marriage or a cut-
down library bookcase.

▲ SECRETAIRE
BOOKCASES
When the deep top
drawer of the
secretaire bookcase is
open the front
"drops" to form the
writing surface. The
fine quality of the
interior will be
reflected in the price –
about £12,000 – a
lesser one might be as
little as £2,000.

MISCELLANEOUS FURNITURE

Antique furniture is not confined to the main types covered on the previous pages. There is also an extensive array of other interesting and attractive pieces, which, although they do not fall into any particular category, are nonetheless extremely popular with antiques collectors.

► MIRRORS

Don't confuse carved giltwood mirrors, such as this one, made *c.*1750, with later gilded composition ones. If rather than wood, you can see a cement-like substance over a wire frame, it's a composition mirror – and worth a fraction of the price. £3,000+

▲ OAK COFFERS

You can still find 17th century coffers for a few hundred pounds. Carving, as here, adds to value; be suspicious of unusually regular and stiff carving – it could have been added in the 19th century. £1,500–2,000

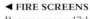

◄ FIRE SCREENS

Because many 17th and 18th century ladies' cosmetics were made with wax, fire screens such as this, provided essential protection from the roaring fires, to stop their make-up melting and dripping down their faces! £400+

◀ BEDS
Nothing can give a more sumptuous look to a bedroom than an antique bed, but before you buy one remember they are often smaller than modern beds so you may need to have a mattress specially made. Nearly all four poster (tester) beds have been changed in some way. Many are composites from different periods. This one has panels dating from *c*.1600 combined with later additions. £5,000

▼ STOOLS
Although the stool is the simplest type of seat furniture, don't expect to find them all at rock bottom prices – they can be surprisingly valuable.

This pair of French mid-18th century X-Frame stools, would be worth over £2,000 – but you could find a Victorian or Edwardian one for much less.

▲ COMMODES
Originally dubbed "night tables" during the prudish Victorian era, cupboards for chamberpots were re-named "commodes" – the name has stayed the same ever since. £500-2,000

Pottery & Porcelain

Ceramics can be broadly divided into two main groups: pottery, which is opaque when held to the light, and porcelain, which is translucent. Within these two categories are a huge range of different types of wares which evolved over the centuries as new manufacturing techniques were developed.

If you're just beginning your collection the multitude of pottery wares produced during the 19th century could be an ideal starting point. During this period the Staffordshire area produced vast numbers of inexpensive household and decorative objects, which at the time cost a few shillings or less. These are still abundantly available and although collectable have remained relatively inexpensive.

Porcelain has long been highly prized and tends to be more expensive than pottery. The field is divided into two main groups, hard- and soft-paste porcelain. Many pieces have marks of some type but these are no guarantee of authenticity because many factories copied each other's marks to make their products more desirable.

Value is usually a matter of size, age, rarity, decorative appeal and, above all, condition. European 18th century porcelain tends to be very highly priced but you can often buy damaged pieces for a fraction of the cost of those in perfect condition.

BASICS

When you first look at a piece of pottery or porcelain, an understanding of the materials and techniques used in its manufacture can help you identify its origin, date and how much it might be worth. The three main factors to assess are:
● Material
● Glaze
● Decoration

MATERIALS
Pottery
This has a relatively coarse texture, compared with porcelain, and is usually opaque if held to the light; the two main types are earthenware, and non-porous stoneware.

Earthenware
Clay fired at a temperature of less than 2200F (1200C) is classified as earthenware. The body is porous, and may be of a white, buff, brown, red or grey colour, depending on the colour of the clay and on the iron content.

Stoneware
This is made from clay which can withstand firing at a temperature of up to 2250F (1400C). The high firing temperature makes the clay fuse into a non-porous body which does not absorb liquids, and may be semi-translucent. Bodies vary in colour.

Porcelain
If it's slightly translucent the chances are it's porcelain; now you must decide which type — hard- or soft-paste. If the body looks smooth, like icing sugar, it is probably hard-paste, if it looks granular, like sand, it is more likely to be soft-paste.

Hard-paste porcelain

A hard-paste porcelain Meissen quatrefoil dish £2,000-3,000

All Chinese and much Continental porcelain is hard-paste, and made from kaolin (china clay) and petuntse (china stone). First the object is fired, then dipped in glaze, then refired. The china stone bonds the particles of clay together and gives translucency. Because the firing takes place at a very high temperature the object attains the consistency of glass.

The first hard-paste porcelain was made in China in the 9th century AD. In Europe the Meissen factory began producing porcelain in the early 18th century, and before long, factories throughout Europe began making hard-paste porcelain.

Soft-paste porcelain

A Chelsea soft-paste porcelain group depicting Winter and Spring £2,000-3,000

As the name suggests, soft-paste porcelain is more vulnerable to scratching than hard-paste. There are several types of soft-paste porcelain, each using fine clay combined with different ingredients to give translucency.

Soft-paste can often be identified because the glaze sits on the surface, and feels warmer and softer to the touch and looks less glittering in appearance than hard-paste. Chips in soft-paste look floury, like fine pastry; in hard-paste porcelain chips look glassy.

Soft-paste porcelain was first produced in Italy during the 16th century. Later factories using soft-paste include St Cloud, Chantilly, Vincennes, Sèvres, Capodimonte and Chelsea.

Bone China
This is a type of English porcelain first made c.1794 using a large proportion of bone-ash added to hard-paste ingredients. This body was used by prominent English factories such as Spode, Flight & Barr, Derby, Rockingham, Coalport and Minton.

GLAZES
Glazes can be translucent, opaque, or coloured. Hard-paste porcelain was given a feldspar glaze, which fused with the body when fired. On soft-paste porcelain the glaze tends to pool in the crevices.

A variety of different glazes were used on pottery and porcelain, the main ones are:

Lead glaze
Used on most soft-paste porcelain, and on earthenwares such as creamware.

A Dutch delftware tin glaze tortoise £1,200-1,800

Tin glaze
A glaze to which tin oxide has been added to give an opaque white finish.

Salt glaze
A glaze formed by throwing common salt into the kiln at about 1800F (1000C) during the firing.

DECORATIVE TECHNIQUES
Decoration can be added before or after glazing. Underglaze decoration means the colours have been added before glazing.

Underglaze blue
Blue pigment, known as cobalt blue, was used on Chinese blue and white porcelain, European delftware, and soft-paste porcelain.

Overglaze enamels
Overglaze enamels were made by adding metallic oxide to molten glass and reducing the cooled mixture, which, when combined with an oily medium, could be painted over the glaze and fused to it by firing. The range of colours was larger than with underglaze colours.

MARKS
Marks are found on the base of many objects. These may include factory marks, which changed periodically and can therefore help with dating, and maker's initials.
● Many marks were copied or faked so marks should not be taken as a guarantee of authenticity.

CHINESE POTTERY & PORCELAIN

Mention Chinese ceramics and many people immediately think of priceless Ming and assume that this collecting area is definitely beyond their reach. In fact, because fine pottery and porcelain have been produced in China for longer than anywhere else in the world, it's not hard to find pieces that are both decorative and inexpensive – although there are of course some extremely highly priced objects as well.

The Chinese discovered the art of making porcelain, in the Tang Dynasty, AD618-906. When Dutch traders began importing

Chinese porcelain to Europe in the 17th century (the late Ming period) no European maker had yet been able to produce such fine quality wares and there was a huge demand for Chinese porcelain – as well as a scramble to find out how it was made (see p62). Nearly all porcelain was blue and white until *c.*1700, when more varied colour schemes such as *famille rose* and *famille verte* were introduced. The many objects made for the European market, often using Western shapes decorated with traditional Chinese designs, are known as "export wares".

Later Chinese Dynasties		
	Liao	907–1125
Wei	386–557	
	Sung	960–1280
Sui	589–617	
	Chin	1115–1260
Tang	618–906	
	Yuan	1280–1368
5 Dyn–		
	Ming	1368–1644
asties	907–960	
	Qing	1644–1916

MING

VALUE DEPENDS ON QUALITY AND CONDITION. PROVINCIAL EXPORT PIECES OF LESSER QUALITY, OR SLIGHTLY CHIP- PED OR CRACKED WARES, CAN BE SURPRISINGLY AFFORDABLE. THIS BOWL WOULD BE WORTH OVER £100,000 BUT YOU CAN FIND PIECES FROM £100.

BEWARE

Don't rely on dynasty reign marks alone for dating Chinese porcelain – as many as 80% are retrospective, and were simply used to show respect for earlier classical wares.

MING OR QING?

Ming patterns were often repeated during the Qing period; Ming pieces can be identified by:

● thick bluish glaze, suffused with bubbles
● tendency to reddish oxidization
● knife marks on the tallish footrim.

▲ BLUE AND WHITE

Chinese blue and white was made by painting the blue decoration onto the porcelain base, before glazing – a technique known as "underglaze blue". Later wares, such as these Qing export vases (worth £7,000-9,000) can be identified by:
● complicated designs
● harder, more evenly applied blue
● thinner glaze.

▲ FAMILLE VERTE

Famille verte ("green family") porcelain is dominated by a brilliant green and was used to decorate export wares from the Kangxi period (1662-1722). £5,000-6,000

▲ FAMILLE ROSE

Opaque pink enamel decorated wares are termed *"famille rose"* ("pink family"). These were often copied in the 19th century by the French maker Samson: crackling in the enamel colours (a fine net-work of cracks) is good sign the piece is authentic. £400-£600

SYMBOLS

The decoration on Chinese ceramics usually has symbolic significance:

Dragons represent authority, strength, wisdom, and the Emperor.

Pairs of ducks symbolize marital bliss.

The peony shows love, beauty, happiness and honour.

The pine, *prunus* and bamboo together denote spiritual harmony.

Cranes show longevity, and transport for Immortals.

JAPANESE POTTERY & PORCELAIN

Japanese ceramics have long been among the most sought after of all Oriental works of art. Although their wares often reflect the influence of Chinese styles, Japanese potters developed their own distinctive colour schemes and patterns. According to legend, the first Japanese porcelain was made in 1616, in the town of Arita, some years after it was first made in nearby China. The wares

you are most likely to come across are Arita, Imari, Kakiemon and Satsuma. Not all of these cost a fortune – you can still find pieces for a few hundred pounds or less. Decoration can affect value dramatically. The plate below is worth over £10,000 because it's decorated with the cipher of the Dutch East India Company. Without this it would be worth £1,500+.

JAPANESE OR CHINESE?

Japanese blue and white wares, such as this *c.*1690 Arita export dish have three distinctive features:

● granular porcelain

● extremely dark (as here) or very soft underglaze blue

● three or more spur marks, on the underside. £10,000+

◀ ARITA WARES
Arita porcelain is called after the town of Arita, where Japanese porcelain production was concentrated. Although Arita, Imari and Kakiemon were all made in the same kilns, the term "Arita" usually only describes blue and white wares.

▲ KAKIEMON WARES
Named after the man who is said to have invented coloured enamelling in Japan, you can identify Kakiemon wares,

such as this dish, by their often geometric shape, white ground, asymmetric, high quality painted decoration, and predominant reds and sky blues. £10,000+

▶ SATSUMA WARE
Satsuma wares are recognizable by their cream-coloured ground, lavish gold decoration, and finely crazed glaze. Prices vary widely – quality pieces may fetch tens of thousands, but you can find single mid-19th century or later pieces for as little as £200. This 19th century vase is one of a signed pair worth about £3,500.

IMARI

OF ALL THE TYPES OF
JAPANESE CERAMICS,
IMARI (NAMED AFTER
THE PORT THROUGH
WHICH THEY WERE
SHIPPED TO EUROPE)
ARE THE ONES YOU
SEE MOST
FREQUENTLY. THIS
LATE 17TH CENTURY
VASE HAS MANY OF
THE FEATURES
CHARACTERISTIC OF
IMARI WARES. £5,000–
8,000

REMEMBER . . .

Remove loose lids from jars
before you pick them up to
examine them.

MANUFACTURE

Imari pieces were
usually painted with
dark underglaze blue
decoration (see p63),
glazed, fired,
enamelled with
colours and fired
again.

DECORATION

Floral designs or
landscapes are usually
set in shaped panels
against the underglaze
blue. Some pieces
have figural knobs.

COLOURS

Colours typical of
Imari are dark blue,
iron-red and gilding,
with an outline of
black. The touches of
green on this vase
indicate its high
quality.

CONDITION

Condition is crucial
to value. However,
damage can usually
be restored and
buying a damaged
piece can be an
affordable starting
point if you're on a
limited budget.

TYPES

Large display wares
such as this vase,
which is designed to
stand on a
mantelpiece, are
keenly sought after;
pairs and sets (called
garnitures) always
command a premium.

FAKES AND COPIES

Imari has been much
faked and imitated.
18th and 19th century
copies are valuable
in their own right.
Modern copies, such as
this Korean vase, may
be expensive but have
little status as
collectables.

EARLY ENGLISH POTTERY

Love it or hate it – the naivety of early English pottery leaves few indifferent to its charms and there are enough smitten collectors to make many of the rarest pieces extremely valuable. During the late 17th and early 18th centuries English pottery underwent a period of rapid development and an enormously varied range of new wares and decorative techniques was developed. Pottery is categorized by the type of body from

SLIPWARE	ENGLISH DELFT	SALTGLAZE STONEWARE
c.1720 SLIPWARE BAKING DISH £15,000+	c.1730 BLUE DASH CHARGER £12,000+	18thC TWO-HANDLED CUP £1,000+
HOW, WHEN & WHERE Made from red or buff earthenware, decorated with white or coloured slip (diluted clay). Zigzag, feathered and marble designs predominate. Produced in Staffordshire, Wrotham Kent, Bideford, Barnstaple, Wales, Wiltshire, Sussex. Dates from 17th-mid-18th century.	Made from tin-glazed earthenware, in Southwark, Lambeth, Bristol and Liverpool. Primitive designs of figures, animals and floral subjects mainly painted in blue white, yellow, green and manganese. Known as "delftware" from Georgian times. Dates from mid-16th-late-18thC.	White Devon clay and powdered flint added to earthenware to make light weight white wares; salt thrown in kiln during firing formed glaze pitted like an orange skin. After c.1745 more use of *famille rose* type enamel colours to imitate Chinese porcelain. Made in Staffordshire, from mid-18thC.
WHAT TO LOOK FOR Dishes and mugs. Named or dated wares, especially those of best-known maker Thomas Toft, who occasionally signed his wares on front – no marks usually. Beware of skilful fakes.	Blue-dash chargers – (plates with blue strokes around edge as in the illustration; often decorated with monarchs); barbers' bowls, pill slabs, flower bricks. Chips are acceptable. Never marked.	Figures and pew groups (very rare), loving cups, mugs, plates, jugs formed as owls, unusually shaped teapots (camels, houses). Usually no marks.

which it is made (such as earthenware, stone ware, creamware) and the type of glaze used (such as tin glaze, salt glaze). If you are thinking of collecting early pottery it's a good idea to learn the differences between some of the most important categories. Below are six types of pottery made before c.1770 (for post 1770 see p78), as well as pointers on what pieces you can expect to see and which are most sought after.

WHEILDON	AGATEWARE	CREAMWARE	
MID-18th C PUG £3,000-4,000	c.1745 AGATEWARE CAT £2,000-3,000	EARLY CREAMWARE TEAPOT, c.1760 £1,000+	
Mid-l8thC Staffordshire potter, Thomas Wheildon, developed lead glazed pottery for tablewares and figures; colours limited to olive-green, brown, grey, blue.	Layers of differently coloured clays rolled together, sliced to build up mingled layers resembling agate and moulded into wares. Lead and salt glaze variously used; made in Staffordshire in 18thC.	Coloured earthenware with transparent lead glaze, developed by Wedgwood in 1760s, also made in other Staffordshire potteries and in Leeds, Bristol, Liverpool, Swansea and Derby. May be enamelled, plain or pierced.	HOW, WHEN & WHERE
Well-modelled animals like this dog; unusually shaped wares, candlestick figures, cow creamers, cottages with figures. Table wares are less expensive. Never marked.	Cats, as shown, teawares, jugs, coffee and chocolate pots, shell shaped wares – inspired by contemporary silver; pieces with more than two differently coloured clays. Never marked.	Red and black enamelling by Robinson & Rhodes; wares marked "Wedgwood"; pierced wares which may be marked "Leeds Pottery". Moulded pieces such as cruets and centrepieces. Few creamwares are marked.	WHAT TO LOOK FOR

CONTINENTAL POTTERY

Most Continental pottery was made from an earthenware base, covered with a glaze to which tin oxide had been added, and is known as tin glaze. Tin-glaze pottery is given different names according to its country of origin. In Italy and Spain it is called *maiolica,* in France and Germany it is known as *faïence,* and in the Netherlands as Delft.

The richly coloured designs and motifs of Continental pottery of the 17th and 18th centuries provided a popular source of inspiration for makers in the 19th century and later. Most of these later copies are highly decorative and collectable in their own right.

► SPANISH MAIOLICA
Shiny metallic lustre decoration, as on this rare 15th century dish, is a characteristic of Spanish pottery. Similar pieces were reproduced in Italy in the late 19th century by the Cantagalli factory – these copies were originally marked with a singing cockerel on the base. £8,000-12,000

▲ DRUG JARS
Maiolica apothecaries' drug jars were made both for display and for storage – hence their colourful decoration. Shapes vary according to the jar's original contents. Wet drugs were stored in bulbous jars with spouts like this, dry drugs were usually stored in cylindrical ones. £7,000-10,000

▲ FRENCH FAÏENCE
This well-painted 18th century plate was made by one of the most prominent French factories – that of the Veuve (widow) Perrin. Many wares from this factory are marked "VP", but the mark is also seen on copies, so don't rely on the mark alone and always check the quality of the painting. £700-900

◄ DUTCH DELFT
Tulips were a Dutch obsession and Delft tulip vases were made in simple cushion shapes like this. Others resembled elaborate pagodas, standing several feet tall. £4,000-6,000

BEWARE
Some genuine pieces of *maiolica, faïence* and Delft have fake inscriptions to make them seem more valuable: be suspicious if the calligraphy seems to lack fluidity and if you see any grey specks in unglazed areas – a sign the piece has been refired.

COPIES

Many honest copies were made in the 19th century, marked by makers such as Doccia, Molaroni, Maiolica Artistica Pesarese and Bruno Buratti – these are collectable but considerably less valuable.

CONDITION

Don't expect to find early *maiolica* in perfect condition, chips and cracks are commonplace and pieces are still valuable despite damage. The rim of this tazza is replaced in parts but it is still worth over £10,000 because the painting is of such high quality. You can find smaller, less finely painted pieces from about £500.

ITALIAN *MAIOLICA*

THE SURFACE OF VALUABLE *ISTORIATO* (STORY) DISHES, SUCH AS THIS 16TH CENTURY URBINO TAZZA, ARE USED LIKE THE CANVAS OF A PAINTING TO SHOW A MYTHOLOGICAL OR RELIGIOUS SUBJECT – THIS PICTURE OF REBECCA AND ISAAC IS TAKEN FROM A RAPHAEL DRAWING.

COLOURS

As in most Italian *maiolica*, the colours that predominate are blue, yellow, orange, black and green. If a wider range of colours is used it may indicate the piece is of higher quality.

CONTINENTAL PORCELAIN FIGURES

Ask any collector to name a European porcelain factory and the chances are the first one they'll think of will be Meissen. This factory is famous because it was the first in Europe to discover the secret of making hard-paste porcelain (in the early 18th century) and because of the exceptionally high quality of its products.

Meissen began to concentrate on producing figures from c.1730, following the arrival of a young sculptor named Johann Joachim Kandler. Before long, Kandler's figures became even more popular than Meissen tablewares. As other porcelain factories sprang up throughout Europe, they too began producing figures in the style of Meissen – some of them even using the Meissen crossed swords mark to make their pieces more tempting.

If you're a new collector you may find the differences between the figures made by the various factories are often so small as to be easily overlooked. But as you become more experienced, details such as the modelling, the shape of a base, the colours and the glaze can tell you by whom and when a piece was made. Don't be afraid to pick the figures up and look underneath for marks – but remember to support them well in your hand when you do!

◀ **MEISSEN**
You may think this twisting figure of Harlequin, made c.1740, looks as if it's about to topple over – but the turning pose is typical of the best Meissen figures which are always full of movement. £15,000–20,000

REMEMBER . . .
Crossed swords alone don't mean you have a piece of Meissen – this is the most commonly faked mark and was copied by Worcester, Minton, Bow and Derby – among others!

▶ **VIENNA**
The different colours on a figure can tell you where it was made. The combination of strong green, pale mauve, puce, and yellow on this group is typical of many c.1760–70 Vienna figures. £3,000–4,000

▲ **FRANKENTHAL**
Frankenthal figures, such as this are often of high quality despite their rather stiff poses. Features typical of Frankenthal are:
● large hands
● doll-like faces
● arched edge to bases
● tufts of green moss.
£1,500–2,000

IS IT MEISSEN?

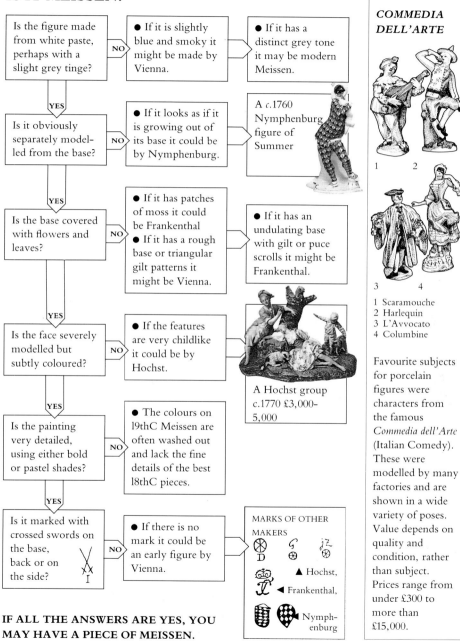

Is the figure made from white paste, perhaps with a slight grey tinge?

NO → ● If it is slightly blue and smoky it might be made by Vienna.

● If it has a distinct grey tone it may be modern Meissen.

YES ↓

Is it obviously separately model-led from the base?

NO → ● If it looks as if it is growing out of its base it could be by Nymphenburg.

A c.1760 Nymphenburg figure of Summer

YES ↓

Is the base covered with flowers and leaves?

NO → ● If it has patches of moss it could be Frankenthal
● If it has a rough base or triangular gilt patterns it might be Vienna.

● If it has an undulating base with gilt or puce scrolls it might be Frankenthal.

YES ↓

Is the face severely modelled but subtly coloured?

NO → ● If the features are very childlike it could be by Hochst.

A Hochst group c.1770 £3,000-5,000

YES ↓

Is the painting very detailed, using either bold or pastel shades?

NO → ● The colours on l9thC Meissen are often washed out and lack the fine details of the best l8thC pieces.

YES ↓

Is it marked with crossed swords on the base, back or on the side? ✗

NO → ● If there is no mark it could be an early figure by Vienna.

MARKS OF OTHER MAKERS

▲ Hochst,
◀ Frankenthal,
Nymph-enburg

IF ALL THE ANSWERS ARE YES, YOU MAY HAVE A PIECE OF MEISSEN.

COMMEDIA DELL'ARTE

1   2

3   4

1 Scaramouche
2 Harlequin
3 L'Avvocato
4 Columbine

Favourite subjects for porcelain figures were characters from the famous *Commedia dell'Arte* (Italian Comedy). These were modelled by many factories and are shown in a wide variety of poses. Value depends on quality and condition, rather than subject. Prices range from under £300 to more than £15,000.

CONTINENTAL TABLEWARES

There are various different ways you can form an interesting and attractive collection of Continental porcelain. You might decide to concentrate on the wares of one particular factory, or a particular type of ware, say coffee cups, which can still be bought singly and affordably. Alternatively, you may want to concentrate on pieces with a common style of decoration, perhaps painted with landscapes or flowers.

Whatever you choose, you will find Continental porcelain in a huge range of styles, shapes, colours – and prices. Value is largely a matter of four key factors: maker or factory, style, quality and condition. Identification is usually a matter of recognizing the characteristic features of each factory's wares such as the shapes, colours and type of paste and glaze they used. It is the combination of these factors, together with the mark (if there is one), which can tell you whether a piece is genuine or not.

▶ **CONDITION**
All these unusual Meissen vegetables have had some restoration, and this has reduced their value (to about £600 for the artichoke or the pair of peas). In perfect condition they would be worth about twice as much.

▲ **DECORATION**
Decoration can give away the maker's identity – Middle

Eastern figures, as seen on this plate, are typical of the Paris factory. £1,000-1,500

▶ **STYLES**
Dating can be confusing because during the 19th century earlier styles were often repeated. This Sèvres tea-service uses shapes fashionable in c.1790, but in fact was made in 1837. £6,000-8,000

COPIES

Some copies are very skilful and are collectable in their own right. One of the most famous 19th century copyists, Edmé Samson of Paris, made this copy (left) of a Meissen original (right). You can tell it's a copy by the greyish colour of the porcelain, the heavier weight, and less lavish gilding. Copy £300–500; original £7,000–10,000.

BEWARE

It's a great mistake to attach too much importance to marks, because many were copied – more than 90% of the Vincennes/early Sèvres linked Ls appear on later copies. One way of detecting fakes is by looking at the paste from which the piece is made – most copies are on hard-paste, but the original mark was used only for soft-paste (see p62 for how to tell the difference).

▶ SÈVRES

This Sèvres jug can be dated by the distinctive pink known as "Rose Pompadour" (after King Louis XV's mistress, Madame Pompadour). This colour was introduced c.1757 and probably discontinued after Madame Pompadour's death in 1764. £2,000–3,000

COLOURS

Certain colours are associated with particular factories or periods. Some rare colours increase value.
1 Greyish turquoise: Meissen, c.1770
2 *Bleu Celeste,* Sèvres
3 Apple Green, Sèvres
4 Böttger Green, early Meissen
5 Lemon yellow, Meissen c.1730–50
6 Egg Yolk, Meissen c.1730–40
7 Tan, German and Swiss factories
8 Russet, Fürstenberg, Ludwigsburg
9 Dark Brown, German factories
10 Iron red, all factories
11 Purple, Meissen
12 Claret, Vienna
13 Puce, German factories, mid-18thC
14 *Rose Pompadour,* Sèvres 1760s
15 Lilac, Meissen, 1740–55

EARLY ENGLISH PORCELAIN

Compared with lavishly decorated Continental wares, early English porcelain may seem relatively unsophisticated – but to many collectors this simplicity is fundamental to its appeal.

English makers tended to be much slower than their Continental counterparts in discovering how to make porcelain. One of the first English porcelain factories – Chelsea – was established by a French silversmith, Nicholas Sprimont in 1745, nearly half a century after porcelain had first been made in Germany and France. Wares made by Chelsea were mainly intended for the luxury end of the market and are among the most sought-after of all English porcelain.

Among the other famous names which became established soon after are Bow, Worcester and Derby. The best way of learning how to recognize the wares of different factories is to study and handle as much porcelain as possible. This way you will become familiar with the styles, colours, glazes and shapes used. As with almost any type of porcelain, marks are often spurious – they can be a help but should never be relied upon.

▲ BOW
Bow, the largest English porcelain factory in the mid-18th century, specialized in Oriental-style wares, such as this tureen, which has three features typical of most Bow pieces:
● white chalky paste
● greenish glassy glaze
● heavy potting.
£2,500-3,500

◀ DERBY
English figures are usually more primitively modelled than those made on the Continent and tend to be less expensive. This Derby figure is worth £800-1,200.

MARKS

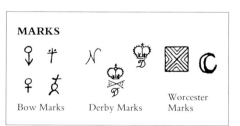

Bow Marks   Derby Marks   Worcester Marks

LOOKING AT PORCELAIN
Never pick a piece of porcelain up by the handle – it might come off. Support the main body firmly with both hands.

▶ WORCESTER
Hold a piece of Worcester up to the light and you should see a greenish tinge, perhaps with small patches of pinpricks. The moulded cabbage-leaf decoration on this jug is typical of Worcester. £1,000+

The shadows given to the insects are a device copied from Meissen and make them stand out more dramatically.

A typical feature of Chelsea is the way the specimens are painted on a larger scale than the flowers.

Chelsea wares can be distinguished from most other botanical plates because the flowers take up almost the entire surface of the plate.

CHELSEA

CHELSEA BOTANICAL PLATES OF THE 1750S ARE CALLED "HANS SLOANE" WARES BECAUSE THE DESIGNS WERE BASED ON PRINTS OF FLOWERS FROM SIR HANS SLOANE'S CHELSEA PHYSIC GARDEN.

CHELSEA MARKS

Chelsea wares are divided into groups according to the four marks used during the life of the factory. This plate, marked with a red anchor, dates from *c*.1752-57.

Triangle period	1745-49
Raised anchor period	1749-52
Red anchor period	1752-57
Gold anchor period	1759-69

Despite a small crack, the high quality painting makes this one of the most valuable types of botanical plate, worth £6,000-8,000.

BEWARE
Fake red and gold anchor marks are usually much larger than the genuine ones.

LATER ENGLISH POTTERY

Not only is the pottery of the 19th century colourful and decorative, it can often provide you with a fascinating visual record of the major events and personalities of the Victorian age. Firms such as Pratt & Co. perfected colour transfer printing from *c*.1840 and pot lids, boxes, plates and other wares were decorated with images of the Royal family, the Crimean War and the Great Exhibition. Royal events such as

Queen Victoria's wedding, coronation and jubilees inspired huge numbers of specially decorated wares. Many of these were once sold for a few shillings but are now avidly sought after. Other highly popular collectables include Staffordshire figures, blue and white transfer printed wares, Wemyss-ware and ironstone. If all these are too expensive, look out for l9th century tiles – you can still find Victorian printed versions for £15-20.

▲ PRINTED BLUE AND WHITE POTTERY

Value depends on condition and pattern: because these three meat plates are all slightly damaged, they are moderately priced, between £150-300 each. Less sought-after patterns start at around £60, the most valuable may be £500 or more.

◄ WEDGWOOD

Coloured objects, such as this 1780s "Jasperware" vase, were made by dipping the object into slip (diluted clay). These wares were made throughout the 19th century and later. The blue used in the 19th century tends to be darker; 20th century copies are of lesser quality. £400-500

▲ DINNER SERVICES

This Mason's Ironstone dinner service is made of a heavy earthenware substance first patented in 1813. It's usually easy to identify wares made by this factory as they're nearly always marked. If the word "Improved" appears on the factory mark it means the piece was made after *c*.1840.

● Large dinner services are especially sought after and valuable. £2,000-3,000

WEMYSS WARE

Wemyss pigs such as this were made in Fife, Scotland, from 1880. There is also a wide range of Wemyss mugs, vases, jugs and jam pots, all of which have risen greatly in value recently. This pig is probably worth more than £400.

WHAT TO LOOK FOR

- good quality painting
- tablewares with red borders – these are early
- figurative subjects – cockerels, cats, bees and pigs
- large pieces.

STAFFORDSHIRE FIGURES

COLOURFUL POTTERY FIGURES, SUCH AS THIS SPANIEL, WERE PRODUCED ON A HUGE SCALE THROUGHOUT THE 19TH CENTURY. SOME WERE MADE IN SCOTLAND AND WALES BUT MOST CAME FROM THE STAFFORDSHIRE POTTERIES, SO ALL FIGURES OF THIS TYPE ARE KNOWN AS STAFFORDSHIRE FIGURES; NEARLY ALL OF THEM ARE UNMARKED.

PAINTING

The detailed painting of the dog's face is a sign of quality and indicates an early date – later figures are more simply painted.

VALUE

Subject matter and rarity affect the price – animals and royal, political and military subjects are particularly desirable. The spaniel would be worth around £800.

REPRODUCTION OR FAKE?

Less valuable Staffordshire figures, reproduced throughout the 20th century, often from the same moulds as genuine Victorian pieces, can be identified in several key ways:

Genuine
- crisp modelling
- detailed painting
- colourful decoration
- finger marks inside – from press moulding
- heavy thick walls
- erratic, wide spaced crackling in glaze
- soft gilding
- kiln grit and glaze on foot

Copy or Fake
- soft definition
- little detail
- little colour
- smooth inside – from slip casting
- thin fragile walls
- regular, exaggerated crackling in glaze
- bright gilding
- glaze wiped from foot

19TH CENTURY ENGLISH PORCELAIN

Various exciting new porcelain-making techniques were introduced and perfected in the 19th century. The development of bone china, which was made from the same ingredients as hard-paste porcelain (see p63) with large quantities of animal bone added, meant that less expensive porcelain became widely available.

Practical, relatively inexpensive dinner, dessert and tea services were made in large quantities, many of them embellished with printed decoration, which was also developed at this period.

You can still buy simple transfer-printed flat wares and hollow wares quite inexpensively. Some of the most affordable collectables are those made by the Goss factory from the second half of the 19th century. Their statuettes and ornaments with printed decoration are available for under £50.

BEWARE

Don't confuse hand painting, which increases value, with a hand-enamelled print (as seen on the left), which is generally less desirable. If it's hand-enamelled you'll be able to see the print underneath the enamel.

▲ PRINTED CHINA

Although hand-painted wares are usually more desirable than those with transfer printed decoration, there are some exceptions. This teapot shows Queen Victoria and Prince Albert – a royal subject always pushes up the price and this would be worth £200-300.

◄ ROCKINGHAM

You may think this is a strange teapot but in fact it's a violeteer – a pot to hold petals and herbs. The highly elaborate moulded and flower encrusted decoration is typical of this factory. £300-500

◄ SPODE

Spode was one of the first factories to use bone china. You can recognize earlier (pre-1830) pieces by their mark, which was usually hand painted – later it was printed. Features typical of Spode porcelain are:
● pattern number in red
● very thin potting
● thin smooth white glaze.
   £1,000-1,500

At the other end of the spectrum, important factories such as Rockingham, Spode and Minton made a variety of highly ornamental wares, often using lavish gilding, elaborate high relief floral decorations and new techniques such as *pâte-sur-pâte*. Value is usually a matter of decorative appeal. Expect to pay more for hand-painted decoration. Any elaborately decorated piece will usually command a premium.

HOW TO DATE 19TH AND 20TH CENTURY PORCELAIN

"Royal" in trademark	after 1850
"Limited" or "Ltd" after name	after 1860
"Trade Mark"	after *c*.1870
"England" in trademark	after 1890
"Bone China"	20th century
"Made in England"	20th century

▼ MINTON

One of the innovations introduced by Minton during the 19th century was the technique of *pâte-sur-pâte*. This involved applying layers of white slip (a mixture of clay and water) to a dark body which was then hand carved to expose the dark ground. The process was a laborious one and pieces were always expensive; this *pâte-sur-pâte* vase would be worth £2,000–3,000.

◀ COALPORT

French designs of the 18th century became popular again in the 19th century. Coalport was one of the most famous factories to produce porcelain in the style of Sèvres. This vase is particularly desirable because of its high quality hand-painted birds. £800+

● Coalport is often marked AD 1750. This is the date the company was founded, not the date of production.

▶ PARIAN

Although this elegant figure looks as if it's carved from marble, it's actually made from Parian, a type of porcelain. Parian figures became popular in the mid-19th century; the best were made (and marked) by factories such as Worcester (as this one is), Copeland, Belleek or Wedgwood and are well detailed. Unmarked figures are much less valuable. £600

Silver

From the earliest times silversmiths realized that pure silver was unworkably soft, and had to be mixed with other more resilient base metals before it could be made into objects.

A silver standard was introduced in Britain in 1300 and all silver objects made after this date had to be tested, and marked to show they contained more than 92.5% pure silver. This marking system has survived in Britain and Ireland with few modifications to the present day. Marks provide the collector of English silver with an invaluable aid. You may come across silver with fake or altered marks, or unmarked pieces, but these are relatively scarce, and once you have learnt to "read" the marks, you will be able to identify where, when, and (often) who made most pieces of silver. Nonetheless, you should always take into account the style of a piece to make sure it is consistent with the date of the marks. Much Continental and American silver was also marked in some way, although in many countries the system was less rigorously applied than in England.

Despite the vagaries of fashion, old silver has remained one of the most enduringly popular collecting areas. Small 19th century objects are still available for £100 or less, and old Sheffield plate and electroplate also offer excellent value.

BASICS

HALLMARKS

There are four main marks:

- The sterling guarantee
- The town mark
- The date letter
- The maker's mark

Sterling guarantee mark

1   Leopard's head
2   Leopard's head crowned
3   Lion *passant*

Silver that is at least 92.5% pure is termed "sterling" silver. All silver objects of sterling quality were stamped with a leopard's head from 1300. By 1458 the leopard had a crown; from 1544 the sterling mark changed to a lion *passant*, shown walking to the left (after this date the leopard's head was used as the London town mark).

4   Britannia mark
5   Lion's head

Between 1697 and 1720, a higher standard of silver, known as the Britannia standard, was introduced. During this period the sterling mark was replaced by a figure of Britannia, and a lion's head in profile.

Town marks

Marks showing the town of assay were introduced by the end of the 15th century. Some of the commonest are:

6   London
7   Birmingham
8   Chester
9   Dublin
10 Exeter
11 Edinburgh
12 Glasgow
13 Sheffield
14 York

Date letters

15   16   17   18

15   1721   17   1781
16   1741   18   1801

Marking with a date letter, which changed each year, was introduced in the 15th century in London, and later in other parts of the country. The letters usually follow an alphabetical sequence, but are unique to each assay office. The letter is contained within a shield.

Maker's mark

19   20

21   22

19 Matthew Boulton
20 John Cafe
21 Robert Hennell
22 Paul Storr

Marks to show the identity of the maker were used from the 14th century. The earliest were pictorial symbols, but from the late 17th century marks increasingly incorporated the silversmith's initials.

ALTERED AND FAKE MARKS

Forged marks

Fake marks are usually less clearly defined than genuine ones; if they have been made by recasting a genuine piece there may be small granulations visible in the outline.

Transposed marks

Marks are sometimes taken from a low value object and inserted in a larger, potentially more valuable one. If you breathe on transposed marks you should be able to see a faint outline around the marks where they were soldered in.

Illegal Alterations

An Act of 1844 made it illegal to alter any piece of silver without hallmarking the additions. However, many pieces were updated to make them more useful, or more fashionable, rather than to deliberately deceive.

PATINA

Over years of use, silver develops a soft glow, or patina, caused by accumulated scratching and knocks and bruises. This patina is important to value. Repolishing old silver on a buffing wheel can destroy the patina of a piece and is usually undesirable.

WEIGHT

Although an item which is heavier than average may not appear larger or heavier, extra weight is usually synonymous with quality, and heavier pieces tend to be more valuable.

STYLES AND DECORATION

Silver styles reflect the taste of the period, and can often provide a good indication of date. Decoration may be applied to the surface or the border of a piece and usually adds to value (see p93 for some of the different types found).

CONDITION

Repairs are usually detrimental to value. If lead has been used in the repair it can be especially unsightly. Areas particularly vulnerable to damage are:

- **Feet:** these can be pushed up through the base with time.
- **Handles:** the metal of the body may be pulled away by the handle.
- **Hinges:** can be broken and are often difficult to repair.
- **Pierced decoration:** may be relatively fragile and prone to damage.

SHEFFIELD PLATE

Sheffield plate, made from a fusion of copper and silver, was introduced c.1740. Most Sheffield plate is unmarked, although some early 19th century pieces had marks very similar to those found on silver.

- A piece with "Sheffield plate" stamped on it is electroplate made in Sheffield in the 19th century, not genuine Sheffield plate.
- Sheffield plate tends to be much less expensive than silver, but the best pieces are keenly collected.

ELECTROPLATE

This method, involving covering a base metal with a thin layer of silver by electro-deposition, was used from c.1840. The base metal was initially copper, but later nickel was used, hence the term EPNS (electro-plated nickel silver). Electroplate is usually marked by its maker, or bears indications of quality.

- Apart from pieces by an eminent maker such as Elkington, electroplate is less collectable than other types of silver.

TEAPOTS, CHOCOLATE POTS &

Tea, coffee and chocolate became fashionable in the late 17th century, and over the next two centuries large numbers of pots for serving these drinks were made.

The shapes of tea and coffee pots can help with dating them, but because many 18th century styles were repeated in the 19th and 20th centuries you need to check the marks on the base to tell whether the piece is a later reproduction. There is nothing wrong with buying, say, a 19th century coffee pot in an 18th century style, provided the marks are correct for the date it was made and the pot is priced as a reproduction. Bear in mind that coffee and teapots were made to be used and may have become well worn as a result – before you buy one examine it carefully for damage, which can be expensive to restore.

MARKING
Teapots are usually marked on the base – it's less common to find marks on the side. The maker's mark on a handle may be different from that on the body, as handles are nearly always later replacements. Lids should also be marked.

▲ TEAPOTS
The "bullet" teapot has a lid with a concealed hinge, which was attached before the base was soldered on. Check lids carefully before buying – if the hinge is weak it may be impossible to restore. £3,000+

◀ DECORATION
Decoration can help with dating. This piece shows a technique known as bright-cutting, which was popular in the late 18th century. £1,500-2,000

WHAT TO LOOK FOR
● Check the point where the handle joins the body to make sure it's secure.
● Examine the hinge on the lid – make sure it is not weak or restored.
● Make sure the spout isn't split.
● Breathe on the finial and around the spout and hinges – this helps to show repairs.

◀ STYLES
Some 19th century teapots were so elaborate it is hard to imagine they were ever used! This one, made in 1814, is covered with undulating foliage and has a handle made to look like bark. £1,500-2,000

COFFEE POTS

THIS 1734 COFFEE POT COULD HAVE BEEN USED EITHER FOR COFFEE OR CHOCOLATE, BUT POTS WHICH HAVE A REMOVABLE FINIAL, WITH A HOLE IN THE LID FOR A SWIZZLE STICK TO STIR THE SEDIMENT, ARE USUALLY TERMED "CHOCOLATE" POTS.

PAUL DE LAMERIE

One of the most acclaimed silversmiths of the 18th century, Paul de Lamerie was a French Huguenot (Protestant refugee) who built up a prosperous London business. De Lamerie's clients included royalty and his most famous pieces were very lavishly decorated.

MARKS

These should be in a line by the handle, or in a group or scattered on the base. Lids should also be marked.

MAKERS

The mark of a well-known maker can add enormously to the value of any piece of silver – this pot was made by Paul de Lamerie, so it would be worth over £30,000; a pot by a lesser name could cost £4,000-6,000.

● Other famous names to look out for are: the Bateman family, the Fox family, Philip Rollos and Paul Storr.

▶ ALTERATIONS

During the 19th century, covered tankards such as the one on the left, became unfashionable and were sometimes converted into coffee pots. Converted pots, such as that on the right, are illegal unless the additions are marked.

MUGS & JUGS

A huge variety of cups, tankards and jugs have been made over the centuries. They remain highly popular with today's collectors. The vast majority of those you are likely to come across today date from the 18th century or later. Although silver is relatively robust, jugs and mugs have often been well-used, and condition is important to value – so examine pieces carefully before buying them.

Other factors which affect the value of mugs and jugs are common to any type of silver – namely quality, date and maker. You will find that a mug marked by a known maker will invariably cost more than an unmarked one, and elaborate decoration will also raise the price – although be careful because many once-plain 18th century tankards (lidded mugs) were elaborately decorated in the Victorian period and these are less desirable than a plain piece in original condition.

MUGS	TANKARDS
BALUSTER MUG, *c.*1740 £1,500–3,000	**EARLY 18TH CENTURY TANKARD** £3,000–5,000

	MUGS	TANKARDS
WHEN AND WHY	Made from the late 17thC, early mugs mirror the shapes of pottery – with bulbous bases and slender necks; those made in the early 18thC had straight tapered sides, later the baluster shape became popular. Mugs became fashionable as gifts in the 19thC.	Most date from *c.*1660–*c.*1780. Made for drinking ale, they became less prevalent as wine and spirits became more popular. Georgian tankards are usually plain, some have armorials. Tankards made in the 19thC (often for presentation) were usually very elaborate.
WHAT TO LOOK FOR	**Marks:** until the end of the 18thC, in a group under the base; later pieces are marked in a line by the handle. ● Check handles and rims for signs of weakening or splitting. ● Examine sides for signs of erased armorials (see p89).	**Marks:** on one side of body or base and on lid; earlier tankards have marks in a line on top of the lid; later they are in a group inside. ● Check handle sockets, they may have become weak. ● Examine thickness of cover – if it's domed, and thin, it may have been reworked from a flat lid.
OTHER STYLES		

BEWARE

Tankards were often converted into more useful jugs during the 19th century. To be legal the conversion must have later marks on any parts which were added – such as the spout. This jug was once an 18th century tankard but was converted and decorated in the Victorian period. Conversions usually have less elegant proportions than authentic originals. £1,500-2,000

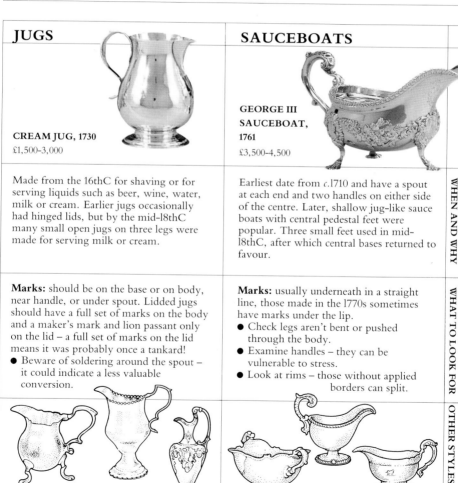

JUGS

CREAM JUG, 1730
£1,500-3,000

Made from the 16thC for shaving or for serving liquids such as beer, wine, water, milk or cream. Earlier jugs occasionally had hinged lids, but by the mid-18thC many small open jugs on three legs were made for serving milk or cream.

Marks: should be on the base or on body, near handle, or under spout. Lidded jugs should have a full set of marks on the body and a maker's mark and lion passant only on the lid – a full set of marks on the lid means it was probably once a tankard!
● Beware of soldering around the spout – it could indicate a less valuable conversion.

SAUCEBOATS

GEORGE III SAUCEBOAT, 1761
£3,500-4,500

Earliest date from *c.*1710 and have a spout at each end and two handles on either side of the centre. Later, shallow jug-like sauce boats with central pedestal feet were popular. Three small feet used in mid-18thC, after which central bases returned to favour.

Marks: usually underneath in a straight line, those made in the 1770s sometimes have marks under the lip.
● Check legs aren't bent or pushed through the body.
● Examine handles – they can be vulnerable to stress.
● Look at rims – those without applied borders can split.

WHEN AND WHY

WHAT TO LOOK FOR

OTHER STYLES

CADDIES & CASTERS

Don't be shocked by the extravagance and cost of the caddies on this page – tea was once so expensive that it was drunk only in the wealthiest homes, and the caddies for storing this precious commodity were intended as objects for display as much as for storage. Caddies were usually kept in the drawing room; some had detachable caps for measuring the tea, while others were even fitted with lock and key to protect their precious contents from dishonest servants!

Nowadays, caddies are keenly collected – and the best ones can be expensive.

Casters played an essential role in fashionable dining rooms when liberal quantities of spices and seasonings were essential to disguise the flavour of stale food. Early casters had straight sides, baluster casters were made from c. 1705 becoming taller during the century. Most were originally made in pairs or sets and today these are always particularly sought after.

▶ **CADDIES**
Sets of caddies always command a premium. This set of two caddies and a sugar box would be particularly valuable because each piece has its original arms and it comes with its fitted box. £8,000–12,000

▲ **CASTERS**
Made to hold sugar, pepper and dry mustard, the shape of casters changed little from c.1705. Better quality ones, such as this, have elaborately pierced covers. This is one of a set of three made by David Tanqueray in 1713 and is worth over £3,000.

▲ **MARKS**
Bodies and lids should have a full set of hallmarks, although early 18th century caddies with detachable lids, such as this one, are often unmarked on the cap. £2,000–3,000

WHAT TO LOOK FOR
This caddy has three key features you should look for on other pieces:
● high quality decoration
● a maker's mark
● date marks of the 18th century – 19th century caddies are usually less valuable. £2,500–3,500

SALVERS & TRAYS

The difference between salvers and trays is that trays have handles while salvers do not. Both were used as presentation pieces and for practical purposes, and good ones are always popular with collectors. Many salvers survive from *c.*1700 onwards, but trays were not made until the end of the 18th century. Those decorated with elaborate borders will probably cost more than simpler ones.

Salvers and trays often had the armorials of their owner engraved in the centre – if the crest belongs to a famous family this can increase value – as well as providing an interesting insight into the previous owner of your tray.

THIS TRAY WAS MADE IN 1806. THE OVAL SHAPE IS TYPICAL OF THE PERIOD. £6,000–8,000

ARMORIALS

Blue (Azure)

Red (Gules)

Green (Vert)

Black (Sable)

Purple (Purple)

Armorials which are contemporary with the piece are preferable to later ones. Many were erased in the 1920s, so check that the metal in the centre is not thinner than the rest.

1690–1700 gadroon border

1730s–40s scrolled border

1790s thread border

c.1850–c.1895 shell & scroll border

MARKS

There should be a full set of marks on the body – usually in a straight line. Applied borders may be separately marked.

◀ BORDERS

Borders used to decorate trays and salvers (and other types of silver) can help you to date them, although many designs were repeated in the 19th century.

FLATWARE

Knives, forks and spoons are usually termed "flatware" by silver collectors. Depending on your budget there are many ways of collecting flatware. Complete services, which usually comprise settings for 12, may seem prohibitively expensive, but odd numbers of spoons and forks in the most common patterns, such as Old English, Fiddle, or Hanoverian are relatively easy to find, and it's often far less costly to build up a service piecemeal. Flatware services do not usually include knives. These often had thin metal handles which may become worn; most collectors prefer reproductions, which are more robust.

► APOSTLE SPOONS

Apostle spoons (so-called because the handle is decorated with the figure of an Apostle), are among the most valuable of spoons. Sometimes they're faked by reshaping ordinary 18th century spoons – you can spot these by the stiffness of the figure. £1,000+

▼ PATTERNS

Different patterns are identifiable by their names; these are some of the most popular ones which have been repeated continually since they were first made. The date of flatwares can affect their price even more dramatically than other types of silver.

1 Rat-tail   2 Old English
3 Fiddle thread   4 Beaded
5 Albany

▲ OLD ENGLISH PATTERN

The most desirable services contain a dozen tablespoons, table forks, dessert spoons, dessert forks and teaspoons. This 77-piece Old English pattern service has the added bonus of a basting spoon and other serving pieces and this will increase its value. £6,000–8,000

BEWARE

Badly worn flatwares are virtually impossible to restore and are worth only scrap value. Only the fork on the left is in good condition. The one in the centre is badly worn, the other has been trimmed to disguise the damage.

CANDLESTICKS

Even though we no longer depend on candlelight for illumination, nothing graces a dining table more elegantly than a pair of silver candlesticks. Most candlesticks and candelabra were originally made in pairs or larger sets. Expect to pay more than double for a pair of candlesticks than for two single ones – even if they're the same design and size! To be a true "pair" candlesticks must be made by the same maker at more or less the same date.

THIS TYPICAL MID-18TH CENTURY CANDLESTICK WAS MADE BY CASTING THE SEPARATE SECTIONS – BASE, STEM AND SCONCE – IN MOULDS. CAST CANDLESTICKS ARE USUALLY MORE DESIRABLE THAN "LOADED" ONES, WHICH WERE MADE FROM THIN SHEETS OF SILVER FILLED WITH PITCH TO GIVE WEIGHT. £3,000+ (FOR PAIR)

BASES
Sheet candlesticks are marked in a line above the base, cast ones are marked in the well, or under each corner.

NOZZLES
Nozzles should have the maker's mark and lion passant.

SCONCES
If the seam on the stem and sconce is not in alignment, the candlestick has been heavily repaired. Here you can see the lion passant mark on the sconce.

STEMS
During the 18th century stems became progressively taller; early candlesticks rarely measure more than 13cm/7in; this mid-18th century one is 25cm/10in.

◄ CHAMBER CANDLESTICKS
These were used to light the way to bed, and unlike other candlesticks, are usually sold singly. This one was made in the 1780s and like many is fitted with a snuffer. £1,000-1,500

▲ CANDELABRA
The separate parts are frequently replaced – four nozzles on this pair are replacements, but the candelabra were made by John Scofield, an eminent 18th century maker, so the price would still be £15,000+.

MISCELLANEOUS SILVER

If you want to collect on a modest budget, the vast array of small novel objects made from silver can provide an ideal collecting area. Look carefully in the display cabinets of a general antiques shop, or at a silver auction, and among the pieces you are likely to find are pincushions, card cases, nutmeg graters, vinaigrettes, snuff boxes, sewing cases, glove stretchers, letter openers, vestas

and sovereign cases – to name but a few! When you examine the marks you'll find Birmingham's anchor mark appears again and again because from the late 18th century silversmiths in this area produced small silver items in their thousands. Usually, the least expensive pieces tend to be those produced during the 19th century, earlier objects are scarcer and can be highly priced.

▶ SNUFF BOXES

The decoration of small boxes has a huge bearing on their price; hunting scenes are particularly sought after – this silver gilt snuff box, made in 1828, would be worth over £1,500+.

▶ VINAIGRETTES

Vinaigrettes such as these were used to contain aromatic salts, vinegar, or perfume and are smaller than snuff boxes, although equally in demand. £1,000-1,500

▶ DECORATION

A piece of silver decorated with a recognizable scene is especially desirable. This Victorian pin tray shows Windsor Castle – one of the most popular views; St Paul's Cathedral or scenes of Edinburgh are also keenly collected. £700-1,000

WHAT TO LOOK FOR:

Silver boxes
- Check the hinge isn't damaged.
- Make sure the marks on the base are the same as those on the lid – if they don't match, the box may have been altered.

BEWARE

Sometimes snuff boxes are turned into vinaigrettes by adding grilles – and vinaigrettes are turned into pill boxes by removing the grilles! £200

▶ MIRRORS

Like most silver-framed mirrors, this one is part of a set of dressing table silver. Its unusually fine quality is reflected in the price – over £100,000 for the set! During the late 19th/early 20th century less expensive mirrors were made from wooden frames covered with velvet and decorated with die stamped silver. These are often badly worn and difficult to clean but still highly sought after.

DIE STAMPING

Die stamped silver is patterned by pressing solid metal moulds together on either side of sheet silver – the technique made it relatively inexpensive to mass-produce elaborate decoration and was much used in the 19th century.

▲ SILVER AND GLASS

Glass and silver are often combined to produce some highly decorative objects, but before buying any silver and glass object remember to check that the glass is not broken as it can be costly to replace, especially if shaped. This 1911 Ramsden & Carr silver and enamel case contains its original glass bottle. £2,000+

▲ ART NOUVEAU SILVER

Silver items reflecting the Art Nouveau style, marked by well known makers or retailers, are becoming increasingly collectable. This box, with its typical Art Nouveau motif on the lid, was made for Liberty & Co. and would be worth £700–1,000.

SILVER DECORATION

Small silver is decorated in a wide variety of ways. Some of the most common terms used to describe the techniques are:

BRIGHT CUTTING: a type of faceted engraving.

CHASING OR EMBOSSING: patterns made by hammering or punching.

CUT-CARD DECORATION: flat shapes added to rims etc.

FILIGREE: open wire panels decorated with little silver beads.

OTHER METALS

Pewter, brass, copper, Sheffield plate and electroplate are just some of the most commonly seen metals that have been used to make a wide variety of decorative and utilitarian objects throughout the centuries. Dating unmarked metal objects can be a potential minefield if you're not sure what to look out for. The style of a metal object rarely provides a reliable way of deciding when it was made because many early designs were copied in the 19th and 20th centuries. Before buying don't be afraid to pick up different pieces to compare their weight: most modern copies are noticeably lighter in weight than genuinely old ones. Look for signs of wear and tear consistent with age: the undersides of objects should be covered with a fine patina of scratches and the edges of plates and hollow wares should be worn smooth. Treat anything with sharp edges or which looks as though it's in perfect condition with suspicion.

◄ **PEWTER**
Pewter, or "poor man's silver" as it's sometimes known, is an alloy mainly made of tin and lead, in varying proportions. Pieces in poor condition are less desirable; this c.1780 flagon has an attractive acorn finial and domed cover typical of the period, and is worth £500-800.

HOW OLD IS IT?

- Pewter more than 50 years old develops a characteristic dull glowing patina.
- Pieces made before c.1826 are usually marked with a maker's stamp and a mark showing the purity of the metal.
- Tavern pewter made after c.1826 should bear capacity marks.

▲ **BRASS**
Old brass objects, such as this George III candlestick, often reflect the styles of silver objects of the same date. Pieces marked with makers' stamps are especially desirable and command a premium; this candlestick is marked by E. Berry, and is worth £1,000-2,000.

◀ SHEFFIELD PLATE
Old Sheffield plate was made from a thin layer of silver fused onto a sheet of copper. This type of plate was used from c.1760 as a less expensive alternative to silver. Although highly collectable, Sheffield plate remains good value; this c.1810 novelty tea urn is worth £500–700.

● You can usually identify old Sheffield plate by its slightly pinkish tinge caused by areas of silver wearing thin, revealing the copper beneath.

▶ COPPER
If you find a piece of metalware marked with a twisted rope symbol you're in luck because this is the mark of leading 19th century manufacturers Perry, Son & Co. This unusually-shaped jug is doubly desirable as it was designed by Dr Christopher Dresser, one of the most influential designers of the Victorian period. £1,000–1,500

▲ ELECTROPLATE
● The technique of applying a thin layer of silver over a nickel or alloy base was developed in the mid-19th century.

● Electroplate is susceptible to wear – you can see where the silver has worn thin on this corkscrew.

● You can have pieces replated but this gives an unnaturally bright appearance which is far less desirable. £200–300.

Glass

Glass is a fascinating and accessible collecting area. Despite the fragility of the substance, glass from the 18th century and later is relatively easy to find, and plain objects can still be inexpensive.

Although the precise origins of glass are unknown; it was made in ancient Egypt, Syria and Rome. The basic material was made from heating and fusing silica (usually sand) with a flux (potash or soda) and a stabiliser (usually lime).

Drinking glasses, made in large numbers throughout the 18th century, have long been popular with collectors. Value depends on rarity of the decoration, as well as the shape of the bowl, stem and foot. Many of the more valuable types of 18th century glass have been faked so always buy from a reputable source, or take expert advice when in doubt.

Colourful glass of the 19th century is also increasingly popular with collectors. Many new glass-making techniques were introduced during the 19th century and colours became increasingly varied. Cameo glass and overlay glass are two of the most attractive types to look out for, although the best marked examples can be expensive. Unmarked glass of the 19th century is still reasonably priced, and 19th century table glass can be less expensive than modern equivalents.

BASICS

There are three main types of glass:

SODA GLASS
Made in Venice from the 13th century. The soda was derived from burnt seaweed, and gave the molten glass a malleable quality which allowed glassmakers to create very elaborate shapes.

POTASH GLASS
Potash glass was made in Northern Europe. The potash was derived from burnt wood and bracken. Potash glass was particularly suited to cutting and engraving.

LEAD GLASS
Made from potash with the addition of lead oxide (instead of lime), this glass, developed by George Ravenscroft, was used in England and Ireland from the late 17th century, and in Europe from the late 18th century. Lead glass is characterized by its weight and clarity and is well suited to cutting.

DECORATION
Decoration on glass can add substantially to its value.

The main decorative techniques used are:
● Cutting
● Enamelling
● Gilding
● Engraving

CUTTING
Cut facets in glass emphasize its refractive (light transmitting) qualities. Cut decoration can help with dating. The earliest patterns were shallow surface cuts. Patterns became increasingly elaborate in the late 18th and early 19th centuries (see p100-101).

ENAMELLING
Painting in coloured enamels was popular on Venetian glass from the late 15th century and became fashionable in England in the mid-18th century.

An 18th century enamelled wine-glass attributed to William Beilby £4,000-6,000

The best-known English enamellers were the Beilby family. There are two types of enamelling.

- **Fire enamelling:** the enamel was painted on the surface of the glass, and the glass fired to fix the decoration. This is the most permanent and usual form of enamelling.
- **Cold enamelling:** also known as cold painting, involved painting the glass without firing. This technique has the disadvantage that the enamelling wears off easily, and was mainly used on inexpensive items.

GILDING

Gold decoration can be applied to the surface of glass in a number of different ways. The most permanent method of gilding is by firing the gold onto the surface of the glass. An alternative method was oil gilding, which involved applying a gold powder or leaf onto an oil base and burnishing. Gilding applied using this method is easily rubbed off.

ENGRAVING

There are four types of engraving:

Diamond point engraving: the design was scratched onto the surface of the glass using a tool with a diamond nib. This technique was used in the 16th century in Venice, and in England in the late 16th century.

A diamond-etched wine glass, Dutch 17th century, £1,400-3,200

Wheel engraving: the design was engraved using small copper wheels of varying diameter which rotated against the surface of the glass. The technique was used in Germany in the 17th century, and became the most common form of engraving in England from the 18th century.

Stipple engraving: a fine diamond needle was tapped and drawn on the surface to form a design built up from dots and small lines. This technique was popular in the Netherlands in the 18th century and is also found on English glasses.

A stipple engraved glass, Dutch c.1745 £2,500-3,500

Acid etching: this technique involved covering the surface of the glass with varnish or grease, and scratching the design with a needle or sharp tool. The surface was then exposed to hydrofluoric acid which etched the design on the glass. This method was popular in the 19th century.

AUTHENTICITY

Fakes of many of the more expensive types of antique glass abound. Victorian glassmakers made imitations of 18th century glass and many fakes have also been produced in the 20th century. These are often discernible in four key ways:

- **Colour:** the distinctive tint caused by impurities may not be present in reproductions.
- **Manufacturing method:** hand-blown glass usually has a pontil mark – a rough bump under the stem – where it was cut from the pontil rod. It may have striations or ripples in the glass and the rim may be of uneven thickness. Later machine-made glass does not have these imperfections.
- **Proportions:** glass has varied in style and proportion throughout the centuries. On old glasses the foot is usually as wide as the bowl. The wrong proportions may indicate a fake.

DRINKING GLASSES & DECANTERS

Compared with ceramics of the same date, much antique glass remains relatively inexpensive. You can still find sets of 19th century glasses for under £100 at antiques shops and general auctions, and incredibly, an antique decanter will often cost less than a modern one.

During the 18th century, large numbers of drinking glasses were made. The variety available means that there are many ways of collecting glass. You may decide to focus your collection on, say, air twists, Jacobite glass, cordials, or gilded glass, or you may prefer to simply collect single examples of each type. Simpler 18th century glasses may cost £50-100, but those with elaborate or unusual decoration can be very much more valuable.

SIGNS OF AGE
● a foot that is wider than the rim
● flaws in the glass indicating it was hand-made
● a bumpy "pontil mark" under the foot
● a greenish or greyish tinge in the glass
● signs of wear on the foot – fine and irregular scratches.

JACOBITE GLASSES
Glasses engraved with roses, doves and oak leaves were made in the 18th century to show furtive allegiance to the Old Pretender (James Edward Stuart) and the Young Pretender (Charles Edward Stuart). Jacobite glasses are particularly collectable but can be expensive – an especially rare one was sold in 1992 for £66,000.

◄ COLOUR TWISTS
Stems with threads of coloured glass are keenly sought after; value depends on the number of colours. This one has blue and opaque white twists, and would be worth about £1,500.

► GILDED GLASS
Glasses with original, soft 18th century gilding, such as this one, are very desirable, but are rarely seen in perfect condition. £500+

BEWARE
You can spot less desirable later gilding, by its harder, brighter appearance.

COLLECTORS CATEGORIZE AND VALUE GLASSES ACCORDING TO THE SHAPE AND DECORATION OF THE BOWL, STEM AND FOOT. THIS ONE IS OF MEDIUM QUALITY – IT HAS A PLAIN BOWL AND A RELATIVELY SIMPLE STEM, BUT BECAUSE IT IS LARGER THAN MOST (MEASURING 23CM/9IN) IT IS WORTH ABOUT £500.

This is a multi-knopped stem, so called because of the series of projections with which it is decorated; some stems have only one knop, which may contain a tear drop of air, other stems are decorated with air twists.

1 Multiple spiral
2 Single series
3 Double series

1 Conical foot
2 Domed foot

The bowl of this 1720 glass is a round funnel shape; other bowl shapes are shown below.

1 Bucket   2 Waisted bucket   3 Conical   4 Bell   5 Ogee   6 Trumpet

This glass has a domed foot, characteristic of many early glasses; others have conical feet. Check the edge of the rim for unevenness, as this may mean a chip has been ground down.

DECANTERS
Decanters were often decorated with engraved or gilded labels describing their contents. This one is made from "Bristol" blue glass – an area associated with coloured decanters, although not all were made there. £250–850

CUT & PRESSED GLASS

Nothing makes glass sparkle more brightly in candlelight than cut decoration, and this is one reason why cutting has long been one of the most popular ways of embellishing all types of glass objects. Early glass was simply cut by hand, in fairly shallow patterns, but gradually patterns became deeper and designs more elaborate, and by *c*.1830 mechanized wheel cutting became the norm. As demand increased for inexpensive glass wares, press-moulded glass, which looked like cut glass but cost far less, became popular. Although 18th century cut glass is increasing in popularity and price; it can still be good value. If you want to collect cut glass to use on the dining table look out for jellies, custards, sweetmeat dishes, fruit bowls and candlesticks; many of these are still relatively inexpensive, especially if you buy them singly.

▶ IRISH GLASS
If you see a piece of glass which looks rather lopsided the chances are it's Irish! Glass made in Ireland, such as this bowl, can also often be identified by its greyish tinge and the typical shallow diamond cutting. £600

CUT OR PRESSED?
Cut glass is usually far more desirable and valuable than pressed glass, and there are several ways of identifying it:

- sharply faceted decoration
- no mould lines inside
- irregular thickness.

CUT GLASS PATTERNS
These are some of the most common cut glass patterns used during the 18th and 19th centuries. However, because they have been repeated in the 20th century, the pattern alone is not a reliable guarantee of authenticity – you should also look at the colour of the glass and for irregularities that show it's hand made.

Plain sharp diamonds

Pillar flutes

Star cutting

Strawberry diamonds

Cross-cut diamonds

Fine diamonds

THE HANDKERCHIEF TEST

Plain early glass has sometimes been decorated with later engraving to make it seem more valuable. To check the decoration is authentic, drop a white handkerchief in the glass – old engraving will look dark and grey, new engraving white and powdery.

● A handkerchief is also useful to reveal the colour of the glass.

▲ PRESSED GLASS
During the Victorian period clear and coloured pressed glass plates were often made to commem-orate important events; this one celebrates Queen Victoria's Golden Jubilee. £30–40

▼ LATER CUT GLASS
Extensive sets of less elaborate turn of the century cut glass can still be very affordable. This is part of a set of 89 items made c.1900; the whole set would cost about £250–350.

◄ ROCK CRYSTAL
Engraved lead glass, cut and polished to simulate the natural facets of rock crystal is known as "Rock Crystal" and became popular during the late 19th century. £250–350

COLOURED GLASS

Coloured drinking glasses and decanters were produced in relatively small quantities in England during the 18th century, but 18th century styles were much copied in the late 19th/early 20th century and some later versions are so convincing that even experienced collectors can be confused (see p98 for signs of authenticity). Most of the coloured glass you are likely to come across dates from after c.1800, when many lavishly decorated glass objects were made both in this country and on the Continent.

WHAT TO LOOK FOR
● Pieces marked by the workshops of Thomas Webb, W.H.B. & J. Richardson and Stevens & Williams.
● Larger pieces.
● Multiple layers of glass.
● High quality design – Neo-classical figures are especially desirable.

◀ OPALINE GLASS
Although at first glance this goblet looks as though it's made from porcelain, it's an example of English opaline glass made c.1850. Much opaline glass was also made in France; quality can vary – the best pieces are made from lead crystal and are very heavy. £300+

▶ CAMEO GLASS
Cameo glass – made by overlaying the base colour with a layer of contrasting glass which was then carved to reveal the colour underneath – is one of the more expensive types of 19th century coloured glass. This large bottle has a silver lid, so is worth £1,500-2,000; but even miniature bottles would be worth £200.

▲ RUBY GLASS
Ruby glass, sometimes made from tinted glass or from clear glass with a ruby stain on the surface, was produced both in Bohemia and England. These two pieces were made in England in the mid-19th century. The value of the piece on the left is high (£2,500-3,000) because of the elaborate silver gilt handles; the jug on the right is worth £400-600.

PAPERWEIGHTS

The most sought-after antique paper-weights are those made by famous French factories such as Baccarat, Clichy and St Louis during the middle years of the 19th century. Patterns were built up from tiny slices of differently coloured rods or canes of glass, set in a mould and covered in clear glass. The size can vary from under 5cm/2in to 10cm/4in or more.

BACCARAT
YOU CAN OFTEN IDENTIFY THE MAKER OF A PAPERWEIGHT BY THE TYPE OF RODS IT CONTAINS AND THE WAY THEY ARE ARRANGED. THIS ONE INCLUDES SILHOUETTES OF A DOG, A HORSE AND A DEER, WHICH ARE TYPICAL OF THE BACCARAT FACTORY.
£6,500–7,000

BEWARE
Reproductions of antique paper-weights abound, but can be identified by their lighter weight.

IDENTIFYING MARKS
Baccarat paper-weights often include signed and dated canes – this one is marked *B 1848*. St Louis and Clichy paperweights are also sometimes marked with initials.

MILLEFIORI
Millefiori ("thous-and flower") paperweights are so-called because their canes resemble a carpet of flowers.

▲ ST LOUIS
Large single flower heads were much used by the St Louis factory. Sometimes flowers were laid on a criss-cross lattice, known as *latticinio*.
£500–600

▲ CLICHY
Clichy weights can often be identified by the characteristic rose they contain. This one would be worth over £2,000 but more common types fetch from £400.

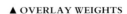

▲ OVERLAY WEIGHTS
Some rare weights, such as this one made by Baccarat, contain a layer of opaque glass through which windows are cut to reveal the design beneath. This one would be worth £3,000 or more.

Clocks

Clocks have been appreciated and treasured from at least the 17th century to the present day. Unlike many other types of antiques, clocks are unique in that they are "working" antiques. You can appreciate them both for their visual appeal and for their technical mastery and they also serve a useful purpose in telling you the time.

If you're a novice collector thinking of investing in a clock, it's probably best to buy one in working order. Most clocks can be repaired, but restoring a "bargain" can be a laborious and expensive business, and unless the problem is very straight-forward it's often cheaper in the long run to buy a clock which has been properly overhauled and restored to working order by a skilled clockmaker.

Most clocks are relatively easy to date and identify because the vast majority were signed by their maker on the dial and movement, and records of most makers have survived. A clock's visual appeal, however, lies largely in its case, which usually reflects the style of furniture of the period.

Despite their popularity, clocks are available at a wide range of prices. Value depends on the maker, movement, case and condition. Plain carriage clocks are available from about £200, a simple bracket clock might cost £600, and a late 19th century longcase around £800.

BASICS

There are three key elements which you should assess before buying a clock:
● the mechanism, or movement
● the dial
● The case.

MOVEMENTS

The movement consists of a system of brass and steel wheels and gears, known as the train. It is usually housed between two brass plates.

The escapement: this part of the movement controls the speed at which a clock runs.

Verge or balance wheel escapement: the balance wheel was used on lantern clocks until c.1670. The oscillating balance wheel releases the two pallets or "flags" on the vertical bar, which engage the toothed wheel. The verge escapement is similar but has a short pendulum.

Anchor escapement: this was first used in longcases from c.1670, and became standard for long-cases and brackets.

Verge escapement

Balance wheel

The anchor engages with the teeth of the escape wheel. Clocks with an anchor may have a long or short pendulum.

PENDULUM

Weight-driven and spring-driven clocks usually have a pendulum to control the clock's speed. The pendulum is a brass or steel rod with a metal disc, or bob, at the bottom. Adjusting the position of the bob on the rod alters the timekeeping of the clock.

DIALS

A chapter ring
B subsidiary dial
C calendar aperture
D applied corner spandrels
E winding holes
F hour hand
G minute hand
H dial arch
I engraved boss
J "matted" centre

The dial is the face of the clock and is attached to the movement by a number of brass "feet". A dial has an important bearing on price. Clocks with replaced dials are much less desirable. There are four main types of dial:

Brass dials: this is the earliest type of dial, used on lantern, bracket and longcases. These have the hours engraved onto a detachable chapter ring.

Painted metal dials: found on most clocks after c.1800. These became increasingly elaborate in the 19th century.

Painted wooden dials: found on English dial clocks, tavern clocks and Continental clocks. If authentic, the wood should show some signs of cracking caused by changes in temperature.

Enamelled metal dials: common on carriage clocks and other types of French clock. They are made from enamel fired on top of thin copper sheet.

HANDS

Early clocks only have one hand (for hours), but from c.1660 most have a minute and an hour hand. Second hands are usually shown on a subsidiary dial. Hands are usually made from blued steel, although gilded brass is found from c.1790. Until c.1740 the hour hand was elaborate; the minute hand was longer and simpler.
● Replacement hands are acceptable if they are in the right style.

CASES

The case houses the dial and movement. Knowledge of materials and styles is useful in dating a clock and in assessing its value.

Wooden cases: these were introduced in the 17th century. Many cases are covered with thin veneers of wood. The most common woods are ebony, walnut, mahogany and rosewood. Wooden cases may be decorated with marquetry (patterns made from different woods see p44),

lacquer, applied metal mounts, brass inlay (on rosewood cases), or a combination of tortoiseshell and brass (boulle work).

Metal cases: Brass is the most common metal; all carriage clocks are brass-cased. Old brass is uneven and shows marks left by the casting process; modern rolled brass is of uniform thickness. Brass cases may be elaborately engraved or decorated with enamel colours.

SIGNATURES

Most clocks are signed, although a signature is not always a guarantee that the clock was made by the maker whose signature it bears. 19th century clocks may be signed by the retailer rather than the maker. Genuine signatures are usually found in the following places:
● until 1690: along the bottom of the dial plate.
● from 1690-1720: on the chapter ring.
● after 1720: on the chapter ring; or on the boss in the arch or on an applied plaque.

BRACKET CLOCKS

Not all "bracket" clocks stood on wall brackets. Clocks of this type were also used for tables and mantelpieces. Nowadays the term is used to describe all clocks with short pendulums and spring-driven mechanisms. These clocks are also sometimes called "mantel clocks" or "table clocks".

Bracket clocks were made from c.1660, the earliest with square brass dials; by the beginning of the 18th century, arched dials became more common. Among the most

often seen English bracket clocks are those with mahogany veneered cases. Large numbers were produced from the late 18th and early 19th century, mainly in London, and you can still find clocks of this type for around £3,000-6,000. Also frequently seen are French 19th century clocks, which were made in a wide variety of shapes. Many of these incorporate such lavish decoration that you may need to take a second look before you realize they're clocks at all!

▼ EARLY BRACKETS

Early (pre-1700) bracket clocks, such as this c.1695 one, are usually the most valuable. You can generally identify them by their ebony or walnut cases and elaborately decorated square dials.

▶ REGENCY CLOCKS

You can recognize a bracket clock made in the Regency period, as it will usually have a convex dial signed by its maker, simple hands made from brass or blued steel, and a mahogany or rosewood case. £4,500

MAKERS

The value of a clock is greatly increased if it's signed by a famous maker. The dial and backplate of this clock (above and right) are signed by Thomas Tompion, one of the most famous English clockmakers known as the "father of English clockmaking," and it would therefore be worth over £100,000!

▲ FRENCH BRACKET CLOCKS

Depending on the degree of elaboration, prices for French clocks start at around £500. This one is decorated with a bronze figure of a negress (representing Africa) and a gilt panther and tortoise and is worth £5,000 or more.

MOVEMENTS
Most mahogany brackets originally had a verge escapement (see p104–105): many of these were converted to an anchor escapement but this should not put you off buying.

STRIKE/SILENT LEVER
The strike/silent lever controls the striking mechanism of the clock and can be used to turn it off without affecting its running.

MAHOGANY BRACKETS
MOST MAHOGANY CLOCKS ARE LARGER THAN EARLIER EBONY OR WALNUT ONES. THIS ONE, WHICH WAS MADE *c.*1785, IS OF STANDARD SIZE AND MEASURES 51CM/20IN. £7,500

CLOCK CARE
- Carefully dust and wax wooden cases.
- Never attempt to clean brass or silvered dials.
- Ask an expert to oil and clean the clock's mechanism.
- Hold clocks upright if you're moving them from one room to another.
- Secure or remove the pendulum before a long journey.

BEWARE
Check finials all match. On many clocks some have been replaced – this is less desirable.

CASES
Both elaborate and simple cases were made from mahogany. This one is fairly simple, but the illustrations below show some of the more elaborate varieties found.

| Lacquer *c.*1770 ht 63.5cm/25in | Mahogany *c.*1780 ht 49.5cm/19½in | Mahogany *c.*1780 ht 52cm/20½in | Mahogany *c.*1795 ht 40cm/15¾in | Ebonized *c.*1810 ht 48cm/19in | Mahogany *c.*1827 ht 66cm/26in |

LONGCASE CLOCKS

Perhaps because of their homely appearance and reassuring "tick-tock", longcases, popularly known as "grandfather" clocks, are among the most appealing of all antique clocks. Most longcases were made in England from the late 17th-19th centuries, although lesser numbers were also produced in Europe and America. The standard longcase runs for 8 days and has an anchor escapement. Like most types of clock, value is dependent on the quality of the case, movement and dial. If a clock has an unusual or attractively painted dial, or an elaborate marquetry or lacquered case, it will cost more than a run-of-the-mill version. Size can also have a bearing on price. Smaller longcases are usually more expensive than larger ones – and for good reason – taller ones were built to fit in rooms with higher ceilings than many homes of today – so before you buy a longcase remember to check it will fit!

DIALS

Originally square, dials became arched in *c.*1720. Most longcases have brass dials, as here, or painted ones, like the clock opposite. Brass dials are usually 30cm/12in in diameter and have an applied chapter ring (the band showing the numbers) and applied spandrels (corners).

QUICK DIAL CHECK

square (17thC)   arched (*c.*1700-19thC)   circular (*c.*1800)

▲ WALNUT LONGCASES
Some of the earliest longcase clocks were covered with walnut veneers over an oak carcass. Cross-banded veneers (a strip laid at right angles to the main veneer) add to value. £20,000+

▲ MARQUETRY
Floral marquetry was a popular way of decorating longcases between 1680 and 1710. Earlier examples have small inset panels of marquetry decoration; on later ones, such as this, the design covers the entire surface. £12,000+

Finials are easily damaged and replacements, though acceptable, are less desirable.

The small dials measure the seconds and the calendar months.

The hands on most longcases are made from "blued" steel – the metal was heated to create the dark colour.

The trunk – centre section of the case – has a door which opens to allow you to adjust the pendulum and fit the weights. Longcases were designed to stand against a wall, so the backs are made from unpolished wood.

The style of the pediment can give an indication of the age of the clock; the broken pediment seen here was popular in the late 18th century.

The painted dial has attractive figures in the spandrels and a moon disc, showing the phases of the moon, in the arch. Look for crazing (a fine network of cracks) on painted dials as this is a sign of authenticity.

NAMES TO LOOK OUT FOR

This clock is signed by a Birmingham clock-maker named Edward White. London makers of long-cases are usually particularly sought after, especially: Thomas Mudge Sr, William Dutton and John Holmes.

MAHOGANY LONGCASES

MAHOGANY WAS USED TO MAKE LONGCASES FROM THE MID-18TH CENTURY UNTIL THE 19TH CENTURY. BECAUSE THIS ONE (OF 1785) IS FAIRLY ELABORATE IT'S WORTH AROUND £2,000, BUT YOU CAN FIND SIMPLE 19TH CENTURY VERSIONS FROM ABOUT £1,000.

The wood on the base and plinth should match the rest of the case. If it looks different parts may have been replaced and this will reduce value.

CARRIAGE CLOCKS

Few people today would think of packing a carriage clock when they go on a journey, even though, as one of the earliest types of travelling clock, this is what they were made for. Carriage clocks usually have brass cases and were fitted with handles so they could be more easily carried – hence their name – many also came with a leather travelling case. Nearly all carriage clocks were made in France during the 19th and early years of the 20th century; a few were also produced in England. Carriage clocks are among the least expensive types of antique clocks available. You can still buy less elaborate models for around £300-600 although quality ones may cost over £2,000.

CHECKLIST OF TYPICAL FRENCH CARRIAGE CLOCK FEATURES
- white enamel dial
- black numerals
- stamped mark or signature on the backplate
- 8-day duration spring driven movement with going barrel
- bevelled glass panels
- blued steel hands.

QUALITY FEATURES
- engraved case
- panelled *cloisonné* or porcelain case
- subsidiary dials.

FIRMS & MAKERS TO LOOK OUT FOR
Auguste (active from 1840) French
Abraham-Louis Breguet (1747-1823) French
Achille and Louis Brocot (active 19thC) French
Dejardin (active 19thC) French
Pierre and Alfred Drocourt (1860-89) French
Frodsham family (19/20thC) English
Paul Garnier (*b*.1801-*d*.1869) French
Japy (1772-early 20thC) French
F.A. Margaine (*c*.1870-1912) French
E. Maurice (active 1880s) French
James McCabe (19thC) English
Soldano (*c*.1855-80) French

◀ REPEAT BUTTONS
Some carriage clocks have a repeat button on the top of the case: when the button is pressed the clock repeats the last hour struck. This one was made by Henri Jacot *c*.1890. £900-1,800

◀ ENGRAVED CASES
Engraved-case carriages are more valuable than plain ones. Look for elaborate, detailed decoration which covers as much of the case as possible. This one was made by Le Roy & Fils *c*.1865. £2,000-3,000

◀ SUBSIDIARY DIALS
Clocks with subsidiary dials are especially desirable. This English carriage has an alarm dial; some clocks also have dials showing seconds or the days of the week. £900

NOVELTY & SKELETON CLOCKS

Novelty clocks, which tell the time in a particularly unusual or intriguing way, are among the most fascinating of all clocks. Most of those seen today date from the 19th century when they were produced by French, Swiss and English makers. The value of a novelty clock is dependent on rarity, appearance and the complexity of moving features, rather than the clock mechanism. Condition is of particular importance, as broken novelty clocks can be extremely expensive to repair.

► MYSTERY CLOCKS

This is one of the most common types of novelty clock. The movement, concealed in the base, rotates the figure slightly from left to right, and this motion makes the pendulum swing, even though the figure holding it seems unconnected to the mechanism. £2,500

◄ AUTOMATON CLOCKS

Automaton clocks are among the most varied and valuable of novelty clocks. This one is relatively simple – it contains a bird which every hour sings a melodic nightingale song, while flapping its wings, turning its head, and opening its beak. £4,000-6,000

► SKELETON CLOCKS

English-made skeleton clocks, in which as much of the working mechanism as possible is visible, are usually far more complex and elaborate than those made in France. This typically elaborate one (with protective glass dome removed) dates from c.1870. It was made by J. Smith & Sons and is worth £6,000-12,000.

Rugs & Carpets

The only difference between a rug and a carpet is size. Rugs are usually small enough to hang on the wall – up to approximately 2m/6ft long – anything larger is usually referred to as a carpet. Broadly speaking, rugs and carpets fall into two main groups; serious collector's rugs, and decorative rugs. Older rugs (over 100 years old) are mainly of interest to the specialist collector. More recently-made rugs and carpets are chiefly of interest to the decorative buyer.

Most rugs are categorized by their place of origin or the tribe who made them. To be able to identify the difference between, say, a Kazak and a Kuba, you need to familiarize yourself with the various distinctive colours, patterns, motifs and weaves characteristic of each type.

The size, richness of the colours, fineness of the knots, intricacy of design and condition are all important when valuing an antique rug. Collectable rugs should be hand-made. To check, look on the reverse – you should be able to see the design on the back as well as on the front. Next, part the pile and look at the knots, if there are loops rather than knots this indicates a machine-made rug of very little interest to collectors. Many types of antique rug cost little more than modern replicas. Woven Kelims and Soumacs can be found for around £300.

BASICS

MATERIALS

The foundation material of a rug (the warp and weft) is usually wool, cotton, or (rarely) silk. The best quality wool is fine, soft and shiny. Inferior quality wool is coarse and lacks lustre.

COLOURS

Colour is one of the most important factors in assessing old rugs. The best colours are those made from natural vegetable and insect dyes.

Natural dyes

Blues and reds predominate in most old rugs. Warm red colours are usually derived from the plant, madder. Blue comes from indigo.

- Sometimes crimson comes from insect dyes such as cochineal. This indicates a date after c.1850 when cochineal was first imported to the East.

Chemical (aniline) dyes

These were introduced c.1890; they tend to be harsher in tone, and are not colourfast.

Chromatic dyes

These were first used in the early 20th century. They can be difficult to distinguish from natural dyes as they are colour-fast, but they lack the subtlety of natural dyes, and come in a wider colour range.

KNOTS

The type of knot used to attach the pile to the warp and weft can help to identify where the rug was made. The quality of a rug is reflected by the fineness of the knots which are measured according to their number per square decimetre (15 sq. in). A coarse rug may have 400 knots per square decimetre whereas a fine one may have many thousands. There are two main types of knot used:

- Turkish, symmetric or Ghiordes; this was used in Turkey and many tribal groups in Persia and Central Asia.
- Persian, asymmetric or Senneh; used in Iran and by some Central Asian groups. The threads can be open to the left or right.

PERSIAN RUGS

Richly coloured and exotic, Persian rugs have long been highly sought after; the finest are made from silk and are among the most expensive of all Oriental carpets. Most Persian carpets seen today date from the 19th and 20th centuries and are either tribal village pieces woven both to trade with and to use or town-made factory pieces, produced specifically for the Western market.

CARPET CARE
Carpets can be washed with plain warm or cold water and a mild detergent. Snow is a good way of removing dust – cover the rug with snow and brush it off and it will take the dust with it!

◄ PRAYER RUGS
Garden motifs recur in many Persian rugs and are inspired by the Islamic notion of the garden of Paradise. Prayer rugs – small carpets used to kneel on during prayer – such as this late-19th century one, show the garden through a *mihrab* or arch. £800–1,800

► KELIMS
Unlike other types of carpets, kelims are flat-woven and have no knots and no pile. The many modern reproduction kelims are identifiable by their bright colours and coarse weave. Old or antique rugs such as this Qashqa'i kelim, which dates from the late 19th century, are finely woven and softly coloured. £800+

▲ CONDITION
This Heriz carpet from northwest Persia has areas of repiling, and the outermost borders at each end have been cut and bound; even so, because it's attractively coloured and a good size – 4.35m × 2.97m/ 168in × 114in – it's still worth over £6,000.

CAUCASIAN & TURKISH RUGS

Distinctive geometric designs are a keynote of many types of Oriental rug made in the region between the Black and Caspian Seas. In this rugged mountainous area, known as the Caucasus, carpets were made by villagers using small looms. Each region has its own distinctive characteristics. Among the most famous and frequently seen Caucasian rugs are Kazaks, Shirvans and Sumaks.

Turkish carpets fall into two distinct groups: those made by nomadic tribal weavers and those made in urban or Imperial factories. Rugs cover a wide spectrum of prices, from expensive silk rugs to cheaper Anatolian kelims, which are still available for a modest outlay.

▲ KAZAKS

Large, bold geometric designs and long fine quality wool are features of Kazak rugs. These carpets are usually relatively small – this one is 150 × 113cm/5ft × 3ft 9in – and is worth £1,500-2,500.

▼ SOUMACS

Soumacs are a type of kelim and are one of the easiest of the Caucasian rugs to identify because they are flat-woven rather than knotted, but, unlike other kelims, are patterned on one side only.

This is a Soumac bagface – trappings such as bags, saddle covers and tent hangings are always popular with collectors and can be surprisingly expensive. £400

KAZAK MOTIFS

Pinwheel Karachov Fachralo Bordjalou

Kazaks are often named according to their distinctive designs. These are some of the most commonly seen motifs.

WHAT TO LOOK FOR

- bright vibrant colours – preferably coloured with vegetable dyes (see p112)
- finely textured weaving
- good condition, unless very early
- complete rugs – cut down ones are less desirable
- a natural patina.

IS IT OLD?

- Check the pile with a magnifying glass. If the fading is soft and gradual it's old; if you can see three distinct bands of colour the rug may have been artificially aged.
- Lick a handkerchief and rub it on the carpet – dyes which come off copiously may be chemical – an indication that the carpet is not of great age.

WHAT DO COLOURS MEAN?

RED	happiness
BLACK	rebellion and devastation
BROWN	plentitude, fruitfulness
WHITE	cleanliness, serenity
GREEN	rejuvenation
GOLD	prosperity
WHITE	purity.

▶ LADIKS
The central Anatolian village of Ladik is renowned for its fine-quality prayer rugs (see p113). This one contains a poetic inscription at the base of the niche. £5,000+

◀ SHIRVANS
Shirvans typically have short pile and small geometric patterns, in which dark blues and strong reds predominate. £1,500–2,000

MODERN RUGS

Modern rugs, such as this Shirvan, are coloured with synthetic dyes which look harsh compared to naturally dyed rugs. Modern Shirvans can also be identified by their longer pile and cotton warp and weft. Although they are still of interest to the decorative buyer they are far less valuable. This one is worth £300–500.

INDIAN & CHINESE RUGS

A prison may seem an unlikely setting for valuable carpet making, but during the 19th century large numbers of woven and pile carpets were made in Indian jails such as Agra, Amritsar and Hyderabad and today these are extremely sought after. Indian carpets often reflect the influence of Persian rugs which were used as a source for some designs. India is also famed for its woven *dhurries* – the Indian equivalent of kelims.

The real and imaginary beasts and symbols of power, wealth and good luck which pepper the surface of many Chinese rugs make them highly distinctive – and easy to recognize. Most of those you are likely to come across date from the 19th century or later and were specially made for the Western market.

VALUE POINTS

- Pile Agras are among the most valuable of Indian carpets – prices range from £10,000–25,000.
- In Indian carpets, white or yellow grounds are usually more valuable than red or blue, which are more common.
- *Dhurries* are the least expensive of Indian carpets; prices range from £500–4,000 for a large one.
- Chinese carpets are less fashionable than Indian ones – at the moment. Those made in the 19th century usually fall in the £3,000–5,000 price range.
- Post World War II Chinese carpets that copy French designs and look less "Chinese" are not as valuable as traditionally patterned ones.

▲ INDIAN CARPETS
Carpets made in India for the European market were often extremely large. A big rectangular carpet is usually more desirable than a big square one. This Agra measures 600 × 424cm/19ft 8in × 13ft 11in. £20,000

▼ CHINESE CARPETS
Traditional motifs seen in Chinese art provided the inspiration for the patterns seen on rugs made in China. The design of this Ninghsia rug was probably adapted from contemporary brocade. £5,000

EUROPEAN RUGS

If you visit a sale of Oriental rugs or a specialist carpet dealer you may be surprised at the large number of European-made carpets on offer. Needlework rugs are among the most popular and abundant of Western rugs. Many were made by ladies of the leisured classes from the 16th century onwards, but some were commercially produced during the 19th century. Designs are colourful and extremely varied; some patterns were adapted from Oriental rugs, others were derived from printed textiles.

Flower-filled rugs from the Aubusson region of France have also enjoyed a huge upsurge in popularity. If the price of an Aubusson is out of your reach, you may be able to find slightly worn small rugs or fragments of larger ones for more modest sums.

AUBUSSON RUGS

AUBUSSONS SUCH AS THIS (MADE *c*.1890) WERE WOVEN ON A LOOM AND HAVE NO PILE. £10,000

PATTERN

The design was built up one colour at a time, each colour woven back and forth only in the area required. When a new colour was added a vertical split was left between the wefts, which was stitched up by hand afterwards.

BORDERS

This border has been cut or folded back; Aubussons were originally made with very wide plain borders and were intended to fit right up to the walls and to be cut around fireplaces.

NEEDLEWORK RUGS

The pleasant floral design, good condition, and unfaded colours are all signs of good quality which add to the desirability of this mid-19th century needlework rug. £5,000

Art Nouveau and Art Deco are two of the most significant movements to emerge in the last years of the 19th and early 20th century. The appearance of furniture and applied arts of this period was dramatically altered by these new styles which swept through Europe, England and America.

"Art Nouveau" derives its name from a shop in Paris, *La Maison de l'Art Nouveau*, which retailed glass and furniture designed by such innovatory figures as René Lalique, Emile Gallé, and Louis C. Tiffany. Most Art Nouveau objects are characterized either by sinuous fluid forms derived from nature; or, particularly in Britain, by simple straight-lined designs with a heavy vertical emphasis.

"Art Deco", named after the 1925 Paris *Exposition Internationale des Arts Decoratifs et Industriels Modernes*, embraces two very different approaches to the applied arts. On the one hand, designers made luxurious objects of the highest quality. On the other, modernists developed clean simple shapes suitable for mass production.

In the middle years of the 20th century Art Nouveau and Art Deco became rather unfashionable but today almost any type of object reflecting these styles is highly collectable, although prices for many small mass-produced objects are still relatively low.

FURNITURE

Art Nouveau and Art Deco furniture cover a wide spectrum of quality and prices. The most sought-after and valuable pieces are large, commissioned hand-made items, by known designers. Smaller functional objects, such as writing desks, chairs and original mass-produced furniture, are widely available relatively inexpensively.

► CHARLES RENNIE MACKINTOSH
One of the most influential British Art Nouveau designers, Charles Rennie Mackintosh usually designed his furniture to commission. The clean simple lines of this chair are in stark contrast to the fluid forms of most French Art Nouveau furniture. £15,000

◄ LIBERTY
Furniture made for the influential firm of Liberty & Co. is usually marked with a Liberty label and though highly collectable is affordable. This dressing table is part of a set which also includes two wardrobes; the suite would be worth £1,500.

▼ EMILE GALLÉ

This small table, designed by Emile Gallé, one of the leading French exponents of the Art Nouveau style, has five features characteristic of most Gallé furniture:

- strong sculptural quality
- inventive design
- fruitwood marquetry inlay
- stylized floral decorative motifs
- a signature.
  £7,000-10,000

WHAT TO LOOK FOR

BEWARE

Pieces marked GALLÉ which lack the originality of earlier designs and are less inventive in their use of inlay may have been made by Gallé's firm after his death. Although collectable these are less valuable than pieces made in Gallé's lifetime.

Much unsigned furniture of the 1920s and 30s, such as this cocktail cabinet, remains relatively inexpensive. Quality can vary, you should look for:

- uncracked veneers
- original upholstery
- pale woods
- dramatic but simple geometric forms. £800+

LUDWIG MIES VAN DER ROHE

One of van der Rohe's most popular Art Deco designs, Barcelona chairs such as this were first made in 1929 and have been mass-produced continuously since the Second World War. Pre-mass-production chairs are worth around £10,000 – ten times more than later versions – and can be recognized by:

- a bent chrome steel top rail with separate sections joined by lap joints and screwed with chrome-headed bolts
- a welded stainless steel top rail.

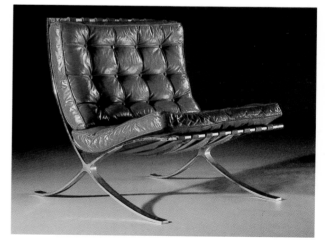

GLASS

Unlike most earlier glass (see p98-103), the value of a piece of Art Nouveau or Art Deco glassware is dependent largely on its maker or designer. This was the heyday of influential glass makers such as Emile Gallé, Daum and Lalique in France, and Louis Comfort Tiffany in America. Designers no longer tailor-made their output of glassware primarily for the dining-table. Glass was in-creasingly used to make a plethora of decorative vases and lamps and, spurred on by the new requirements of "modern" life, designers produced objects as diverse as car mascots, jewellery and scent bottles. All named glass is widely collected, and the best pieces are very expensive, but you can still find unmarked pieces or smaller objects for relatively modest prices.

◄ GALLÉ GLASS
The best pieces, such as this lamp, are made from hand-carved cameo glass (formed by fusing two or more layers of coloured glass, the top layer carved to reveal the colours underneath). Later machine-made versions are less valuable and are identifiable because the carving is not so deeply cut. £15,000+

◄ DAUM FRÈRES
Daum glass, such as this vase, is often very similar to that made by Gallé but can usually be identified by a gilt signature *DAUM NANCY* on black enamel on the underside. £2,000

FAKES
Fake Art Nouveau glassware abounds – among the objects most likely to deceive are:
- "Tiffany" lamps – with fake marks – identifiable because they do not usually have the marked pad on the shade.
- Cameo glass marked "Gallé" – recogniz-able by its stiff, lifeless decoration.

MARKS
Gallé pieces are usually marked with a cameo or incise-carved signature. If you see a star after the signature, the piece was made during the first three years after Gallé's death, between 1904-1907.

▶ TIFFANY
Tiffany lamps have bronze or gilt bronze bases; the shades are made from a lattice of bronze, set with small pieces of favrile (iridescent) glass, marked with an applied bronze pad. £10,000+

LALIQUE

All types of glass made by the most famous glass designer of the Art Deco period, René Lalique, are highly collectable. His prolific output included car mascots, clocks, lighting, jewellery, furniture and figurines. Lalique's distinctive wares were also much imitated so before buying something you think is by Lalique ask yourself the following questions . . .

IS IT LALIQUE?

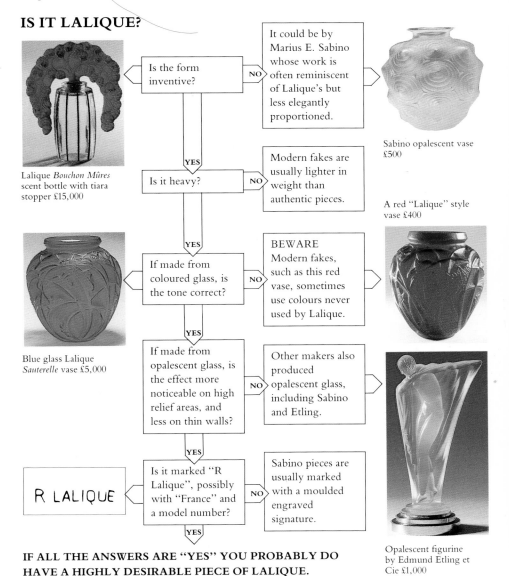

Lalique *Bouchon Mûres* scent bottle with tiara stopper £15,000

Is the form inventive? — **NO** — It could be by Marius E. Sabino whose work is often reminiscent of Lalique's but less elegantly proportioned.

Sabino opalescent vase £500

A red "Lalique" style vase £400

Is it heavy? — **NO** — Modern fakes are usually lighter in weight than authentic pieces.

Blue glass Lalique *Sauterelle* vase £5,000

If made from coloured glass, is the tone correct? — **NO** — BEWARE Modern fakes, such as this red vase, sometimes use colours never used by Lalique.

If made from opalescent glass, is the effect more noticeable on high relief areas, and less on thin walls? — **NO** — Other makers also produced opalescent glass, including Sabino and Etling.

Is it marked "R Lalique", possibly with "France" and a model number? — **NO** — Sabino pieces are usually marked with a moulded engraved signature.

R LALIQUE

Opalescent figurine by Edmund Etling et Cie £1,000

IF ALL THE ANSWERS ARE "YES" YOU PROBABLY DO HAVE A HIGHLY DESIRABLE PIECE OF LALIQUE.

CERAMICS

Whether you prefer the subtle sensuality of the Art Nouveau potters, or the uncluttered modern approach of the Art Deco era, pottery of this period provides something to suit almost every taste. If you're an inexperienced collector this could be an ideal choice of subject to begin with: most pottery and porcelain is marked; wares by the most famous potters are usually well documented; and many pieces are still refreshingly inexpensive.

During the Art Nouveau period the surfaces of plates and vases were covered with floral and organic shapes, or languid, scantily clad maidens, synonymous with the style of the movement. In stark contrast, the clean bright motifs and avant-garde shapes which evolved in Art Deco pottery of the 20s and 30s, evoke equally effectively the spirit of their age.

◀ WILLIAM MOORCROFT
If you see a piece of pottery decorated with raised lines, which look as if they've been applied with an icing nozzle, the chances are it was made by William Moorcroft, at the famous Macintyre Pottery in Staffordshire. This "Iris" vase illustrates the distinctive technique, known as "tubeline", which was made with hand-applied fine lines of slip. £700

► DOULTON & CO
This factory produced such a wide variety of wares that many buyers collect nothing else! You'll have to pay more if a piece of Doulton was made by a famous designer. This vase was decorated by the prominent designer Mark V. Marshall, and would be worth over £5,000; a piece by a less prestigious designer might be worth 10% of that price.

▲ ROYAL COPENHAGEN
The serpentine movement of this group, and the soft pastel shades in which it's decorated, identify this as a typical piece of Royal Copenhagen porcelain. The group, known as "The Rock and the Wave", is so popular it's still reproduced today. Dating can be tricky but different marks were used and these can give a clue as to when the piece was made. £700–900

1894-1900   1894-1922   from 1905

CLARICE CLIFF

The most famous British Art Deco potter, Clarice Cliff, produced such a plethora of diverse shapes and designs that whole sales are now devoted entirely to her wares. Value is largely determined by the rarity of the design. Small objects, or anything in the "Crocus" pattern are usually the most affordable.

Although produced in large quantities, all genuine Clarice Cliff, was hand-painted and you should be able to see brush strokes in the coloured enamels.

FUTURISTIC SHAPES, EXEMPLIFIED BY THIS UNUSUAL *c.*1935 TEAPOT WITH ITS BIZARRELY CURVING LID, ARE A KEYNOTE OF CLARICE CLIFF'S ADVENTUROUS POTTERY. £300–500

Condition is of paramount importance to value and restoration can be difficult to spot. Check spouts and handles for signs of chipping and run a finger around rims and bases to see if they're intact.

The warm yellow "honey glaze" gives the background an ivory colour seen on many Clarice Cliff wares.

Most pieces are marked with a printed mark and facsimile signature.

Decoration is often outlined in black.

FAKES

The many reproductions and fakes can usually be distinguished by their inferior colour and design. This jug looks washed out compared with the vibrant colours in the teapot, and the handle is too thin.

DESIRABLE DESIGNS

- *Age of Jazz* figures
- Wall masks
- *Inspiration* design pieces
- *Circus* series – designed by Dame Laura Knight
- Graham Sutherland designs
- Frank Brangwyn circular plaques.

SCULPTURE

As sculpture, which had hitherto been rather expensive, enjoyed an upsurge of popularity in the early 20th century, inexpensive small-scale figures epitomizing the Art Nouveau and Deco styles became widely available. The female form is a recurring subject; Art Nouveau sculpture shows women in dreamy poses, or draped across functional objects such as lamps. Sculpture of the Art Deco era reflects the dizzy jazz age, depicting elegant ladies playing golf, dancing and smoking.

◀ GUSTAV GURSCHNER
Form, function and decoration are typically intermingled in this bizarre c.1900 bronze nautilus shell lamp by Bavarian sculptor, Gustav Gurschner. Similar fluid shapes were favoured by French sculptors; English pieces are usually less stylized. £3,000

▶ FERDINAND PREISS
The most valuable Art Deco sculptures are usually those made from "chryselephantine" – a combination of bronze and ivory. This one dates from the 1930s and was made by Ferdinand Preiss, one of the most famous sculptors of such figures. £4,000

BEWARE
Many less valuable Art Deco figures were made from patinated bronze – a bronze spelter (zinc alloy) base – combined with ivorene (simulated ivory usually made from plastic). To identify spelter scratch the metal underneath – a yellow colour means it's made from bronze; a silver tone shows it's spelter and far less valuable.

▲ DEMÈTRE CHIPARUS
The bases of Art Deco sculptures are integral to the composition and can provide a clue to the identity of the maker. The architectural quality of the base of this figure is typical of Chiparus. £9,000

SCULPTURE CARE
The patination of a bronze is fundamental to its appeal. **Never** polish a bronze or you will seriously reduce its value.

POSTERS

The growth of the Art Nouveau movement coincided with the development of increasingly versatile lithographic printing techniques. Prominent artists such as Alphonse Mucha, Jules Chéret and Adolphe J. M. Cassandre exploited the media with unrivalled originality. Advertising posters were produced in prolific quantities and nowadays these are keenly collected. The designer, aesthetic appeal, and condition of a poster, will all influence value.

PRINTING TECHNIQUES

ENGRAVING – copperplate incised with design, inked and printed.

ETCHING – copperplate coated with wax into which design is scratched, inked and printed.

LITHOGRAPH – design drawn on stone and fixed; different colour areas are treated with ink-resistant chemical, stone inked and printed.

PHOTOGRAVURE – image photographed, negative applied to plate which is etched or engraved.

▼ ALPHONSE MUCHA
Mucha's posters usually combine a romanticized female figure with elaborate details such as flora and drapery. £3,000

LE FIGARO

NEW YORK
VIA
LE HAVRE ET SOUTHAMPTON
Cⁱᵉ Gⁱᵉ TRANSATLANTIQUE

IS IT OLD?

Art Nouveau and Art Deco Posters have been much reproduced in recent years; reproductions are identifiable by:
● thicker, usually glossy modern paper
● colour printing made up from tiny dots you can see with a magnifying glass – authentic lithographs have flat areas of colour.

▲ JULES CHÉRET
Many posters were printed on cheap paper and have suffered from foxing, tearing, fading or staining. Avoid those that are badly damaged or glued to a backboard. This Chéret poster is in unusually good condition. £900

▲ J. M. CASSANDRE
Art Deco posters are usually strikingly simple and focus on a single dominant image, with strong emphasis on lettering. This poster for the liner *Normandie* is the most valuable of the posters designed by the famous French artist Cassandre. £6,000

Although many old textiles are too delicate to use for their original purposes, you can often treat them as you would a picture and hang them on your walls – and this is one reason why in recent years textiles have enjoyed a huge increase in popularity.

Because of their inherent fragility, age and condition are fundamental to the value of all antique textiles. Among the earliest and most valuable English textiles are stumpwork pictures made in the 17th century. These raised, embroidered pictures often contain amazing inconsistencies of scale – figures may be dwarfed by gigantic insects, huge flowers loom over tiny houses – but this is all part of their naive charm.

Textiles made in the 19th century and early 20th century tend to be widely available and far less expensive. Those made in the Middle East, China, Japan and India are often especially colourful. European tapestries of this period often imitate earlier styles, but with a brighter range of colours. If a whole tapestry is beyond your budget you could buy a small fragment or a chair cover and make a cushion from it. There is also an abundance of samplers, shawls and lace from which to choose. These may vary in price from £50 up to several hundred.

EMBROIDERY

Throughout the centuries sewing was an important pastime for ladies and children. Some multi-patterned embroideries served as a visual recipe book of different stitches. In general, the finer the stitching and the brighter the colours the more desirable the piece will be. Silk embroideries are usually more valuable than those sewn in wool. Because 19th century textiles are relatively abundant, it's best to avoid badly damaged pieces, unless they're particularly unusual.

▲ STUMPWORK Stumpwork embroidery incorporates distinctive areas of raised decoration, formed by padding certain areas of the design. Even though this *c.*1660 stumpwork picture has had some restoration to the ivory silk background, it would still be worth £1,500-2,000.

SAMPLER CARE
- As with any textile, samplers are vulnerable to fading and should be hung away from strong sunlight.
- If you're storing them in a drawer make sure they're well protected from moths – use plenty of moth balls.

▼ SUSANIS
According to legend, embroidered *Susanis* (the word means stitch or needle in Persian), such as this one from Bokhara, were laboriously stitched by young girls before they were married. They were used as a covering for the bridal bed and ripped in half when the bride lost her virginity! £800–1,500

▲ BERLIN WOOLWORK
Berlin woolwork pictures such as this, were made in large numbers in the mid-19th century. Subjects vary enormously and can affect price. This one shows a scene taken from a Sir Walter Scott novel and is worth about £200–500. Pictures of birds and dogs are always popular and can cost £600–1,000.

► SAMPLERS
This sampler is worked in brightly coloured silks; typically it contains the name of the person who made it – Mary Read – and the date – 1838. £400–600

WHAT TO LOOK FOR
- Desirable subjects such as: houses, alphabets, birds, insects, flowers.
- Samplers worked with wool rather than silk
- Reasonable condition – avoid 19th century samplers if they're badly damaged or have holes.

WOVEN TEXTILES

In draughty 17th and 18th century interiors, tapestry hangings provided an essential source of warmth. It was only as wallpaper became popular, and houses warmer, that tapestries dwindled in popularity. Nowadays, although no longer essential, tapestries have once again become fashionable, and collectable. Not all are prohibitively expensive; you can find small snippets of

◀ TAPESTRY
This 19th century Beauvais tapestry is so finely woven that you could easily mistake it for an oil painting – a sign that it's of the highest quality. The elaborate border is copied from picture frames of the period and the design is after a painting by the 18th century artist François Boucher. £5,000

◀ TAPESTRY CUSHIONS
Tapestry cushions are often fragments of a larger piece; this one uses 17th century tapestry which was probably once part of the border of a large panel. Like most cushions of this type, it's mounted on fabric of a much later date. £400–600

WHAT TO LOOK FOR

● rich dark colours, predominantly reds and oranges, gold, turquoise, green and black.
● heavy, rich, soft woollen cloth enriched with silk
● complex designs inspired by Indian motifs
● generous size – 272 × 145cm (107in × 57in) is average, some measure more than 381 × 192cm (150in × 76in).

▶ PAISLEY SHAWLS
Paisley shawls such as this became popular because the voluminous crinoline skirts which were fashionable in the mid-19th century made it impossible for ladies to wear coats! Named after the town of Paisley in Scotland, these shawls were also produced in Edinburgh, Norwich and France. £400

flowery Aubusson, or finely woven Beau-vais tapestry for quite modest sums. Look out for door hangings (*portières*) and seat covers, or fragments of large tapestries, as these are often surprisingly inexpensive.

If the grandeur of tapestry is too over-powering for your taste you might find the homely charm of an antique quilt or the delicacy of antique lace more appealing.

Quilts usually date from the 19th and early 20th century and have become popular with collectors in Europe and America, where many of the finest were made.

Most lace seen today is machine-made, and dates from the late 18th century onwards. Hand-made lace has an appealing irregularity in its appearance, and early pieces are particularly valuable.

► **LOOKING AFTER LACE**
● Early lace, such as this 18th-century flounce, was usually made from linen, a robust fibre, so pieces can be framed and hung on a wall.
● Never display lace by pinning it – rust stains are very difficult to remove.
● Store lace between sheets of acid free tissue paper.£2,500

▼ **DATING A QUILT**
Newspaper or scrap paper templates were often used to stiffen the fabric patches in old quilts such as this American one. You might find laundry lists, letters, or news stories – and these can indicate the date and maker of the quilt.
£1,000–3,000

Dolls have been played with and treasured by children both rich and poor from the earliest times to the present day. Most dolls are categorized by collectors according to the medium of the head (which is often different from that of the body). Among the most valuable dolls are those made from wood in the 18th century and from bisque in the 19th century; both types can fetch several thousand pounds at auction. But you don't have to spend a fortune to build up an interesting collection of dolls. Composition (a substance similar to *papier mâché*), wax over composition and fabric dolls are far less expensive.

Clothes may add to the value of any doll. Some had extremely elaborate wardrobes and those in their original costumes command a premium. However, don't ignore badly dressed or even naked dolls. If your doll hasn't a thing to wear, one way of boosting her value is to buy her a new outfit!

Teddy bears are a relatively recent addition to the collector's market. The jointed bear was only invented at the turn of the 20th century. The most sought-after bears are those made by Steiff, the premier maker of German bears. English bears of the 1930s and later tend to be more affordable, although equally appealing.

DOLL TYPES

During the 19th and 20th centuries many new doll-making techniques evolved; media as varied as *papier mâché*, parian, rag, celluloid, wax, plastic and vinyl were all used for doll-making. Because the range is so extensive, collectors often choose to focus their collections on dolls of a particular type. The table below highlights four categories of doll. By no means all the dolls featured are very old or priceless – as you can see, even a Barbie or a Sindy can be collectable!

Bisque dolls are the largest group of collector's dolls and are covered on the following two pages.

HEAD TYPES

Dolls are classified according to their head type; these illustrations show some of the most common types:

Shoulder head

Swivel head

Open head

Solid domed head

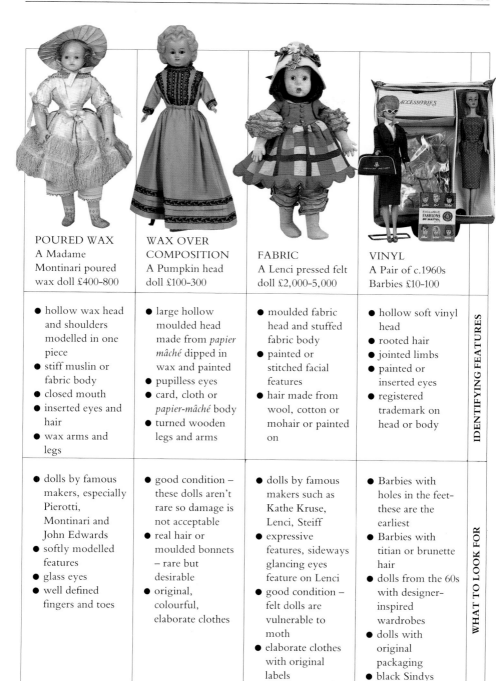

POURED WAX	WAX OVER COMPOSITION	FABRIC	VINYL	
A Madame Montinari poured wax doll £400-800	A Pumpkin head doll £100-300	A Lenci pressed felt doll £2,000-5,000	A Pair of c.1960s Barbies £10-100	
• hollow wax head and shoulders modelled in one piece • stiff muslin or fabric body • closed mouth • inserted eyes and hair • wax arms and legs	• large hollow moulded head made from *papier mâché* dipped in wax and painted • pupilless eyes • card, cloth or *papier-mâché* body • turned wooden legs and arms	• moulded fabric head and stuffed fabric body • painted or stitched facial features • hair made from wool, cotton or mohair or painted on	• hollow soft vinyl head • rooted hair • jointed limbs • painted or inserted eyes • registered trademark on head or body	IDENTIFYING FEATURES
• dolls by famous makers, especially Pierotti, Montinari and John Edwards • softly modelled features • glass eyes • well defined fingers and toes	• good condition – these dolls aren't rare so damage is not acceptable • real hair or moulded bonnets – rare but desirable • original, colourful, elaborate clothes	• dolls by famous makers such as Kathe Kruse, Lenci, Steiff • expressive features, sideways glancing eyes feature on Lenci • good condition – felt dolls are vulnerable to moth • elaborate clothes with original labels	• Barbies with holes in the feet– these are the earliest • Barbies with titian or brunette hair • dolls from the 60s with designer-inspired wardrobes • dolls with original packaging • black Sindys	WHAT TO LOOK FOR

BISQUE DOLLS

Bisque dolls, with heads made from un-glazed, tinted porcelain, are among the most elaborate and valuable of all collector's dolls. The finest French bisques, made by leading makers such as Jumeau, Bru, Gaultier and Steiner, were expensive status symbols even when first made, and remained very much the province of pampered children from the most affluent homes. The earliest French bisques resembled fashionable ladies and came equipped with wardrobes of elaborate clothes, based on fashion plates of the day. Later in the century, the firm of Jumeau began making dolls with child-like features, large eyes and chubby bodies known as bébés – these soon became enormously

popular, and although German manu-facturers followed suit and produced their own child dolls they could never quite match the quality of the French bébé. German manufacturers eventually recovered the lion's share of the market in the early 20th century, when they introduced realistic "character" dolls, with crying, laughing, frowning and smiling faces.

The price of bisque dolls ranges from thousands of pounds to a few hundred and is dependent on the maker, condition and quality, and on details such as the rarity of the mould number (the number on the back of the head which showed which mould was used) as well as the type of mouth (closed is best), eyes, and body.

▼ **GAULTIER
FASHION DOLL**
Fashion dolls can be dated by the shape of their bodies, which were made to fit the costumes of the day. This François Gaultier doll has a narrow waist and broad hips and shoulders well-suited to her bustle dress – which was fashionable c.1870.
£1,500–2,000

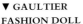

◄ **JUMEAU DOLL**
The *crème de la crème* of collector's dolls, Jumeaus, such as this bébé, are worth as much as £2–5,000. You can recognize a Jumeau by its pale-coloured bisque and large glass eyes.

Many bisque-headed dolls have composition bodies and limbs which are prone to damage (detail left). Slight wear is acceptable and you should only repaint a doll as a last resort.

GERMAN CHARACTER DOLLS

THIS BISQUE-HEADED DOLL, MADE BY ERNST HEUBACH C.1914, HAS AN EXPRESSIVE FACE TYPICAL OF GERMAN CHARACTER DOLLS. SHE IS OF MEDIUM QUALITY AND WOULD BE WORTH £2-500.

The value is reduced because the doll has a replacement wig – original wigs are preferable.

This body is known as a "five piece bent limb" body, because the arms and legs are realistically bent.

OTHER MARKS TO LOOK FOR

$S15H$
939
Simon & Halbig
(active c.1869-1930)

HEU:
BACH
Gerbruder Heubach
(active 1820-1945)

Made in Germany
Armand Marseille.
Armand Marseille
(active
1885-1930)

J.D.K.
Made in 13 Germany
Kestner & Co
(active 1816-1930)

Most bisque dolls have hand-painted eyebrows – delicately feathered brows like this are a sign of quality.

Open mouths were introduced in c.1900. Although more expensive at the time, nowadays dolls with closed mouths are more valuable than those with open ones.

GOOGLIE DOLLS

Some character dolls have very distinctive features and expressions. Dolls such as this, with roguish expressions, large round eyes and impish smiles, and known as "Googlies", are among the most sought after of character dolls. This one would be worth £2,000+.

This doll is wearing her original clothes which adds to her value. If you need to replace your doll's clothes you can sometimes find old baby clothes to fit larger dolls, or use old fabric to make suitable replacements.

TEDDY BEARS

Teddy bears have enjoyed a huge increase in popularity in recent years. The earliest bears were made by the Steiff company in Germany at the beginning of the 20th century. This well-known company was founded by Margarete Steiff who was crippled by polio and confined to a wheel chair as a child. With their pointed snouts, long arms and feet and humped backs, early Steiff bears look much more like real bears than most teddies of today, and are the most valuable of all collector's bears.

Bears are called "Teddies" thanks to the American Ideal Toy Company. Morris Michtom, the company's founder, was inspired by a cartoon showing President Theodore Roosevelt sparing the life of a grizzly bear. The cartoon was so popular that bears became adopted as the President's mascot, and Michtom reputedly wrote to ask his permission to call the bears he was making "Teddy". The President agreed and bears have been known as Teddy ever since.

As bears became more and more popular they were produced by increasing numbers of toy companies on both sides of the Atlantic. In England prominent companies such as Chad Valley, Merrythought, Dean's Rag Book, Chiltern and J. K. Farnell enjoyed considerable success with their high quality products.

Few bears were made during World War II, but after the War production resumed once more, although the appearance of bears subtly changed, becoming less realistic and more like the cartoon bears of today.

The most valuable bears are early examples, in good condition, made by famous makers. In general, Steiff bears remain the most valuable of all teddies because of their unique historical appeal and exceptionally high quality.

ENGLISH MAKERS

Several prominent English manufacturers of teddy bears prospered from c.1915 onwards. Most English bears were originally marked on fabric labels stitched to the foot:

◀ CHAD VALLEY
Chad bears date from the 1920's. Early bears were made of luxuriant mohair, usually gold coloured, with soft kapok stuffed limbs. £200-500

▶ MERRYTHOUGHT
Bears were made from the 1930's; this one has large round ears and joined claws which are typical of this maker. £200-500

▼ J.K.FARNELL & CO.
Farnells supplied teddy bears to Harrods during the 1920s. Winnie the Pooh was reputedly made by this company. The angled ears and large amber glass eyes of this c.1918 bear are typical of this maker. £300-1,300

STEIFF BEARS

THIS c.1908 BEAR IS THE MOST COMMONLY SEEN TYPE OF STEIFF BEAR. THE HUMPED BACK IS TYPICAL OF EARLY STEIFFS. LATER BEARS HAVE LESS PROMINENT HUMPS.

£1,000-2,000

BEWARE

Early bears had glass or shoebutton eyes, attached by wires which can come loose; old bears should therefore not be left within the reach of young children.

Steiff bears were marked with a distinctive button in the ear. Early buttons had an elephant logo or were plain. Later buttons had the word "Steiff" written on them.

The long curved limbs and large oval felt paws with narrow wrists and ankles are characteristic of Steiff bears.

BEAR CARE

- Holes can be mended without reducing value but use similar fabric for patches.
- Dirty bears need specialist cleaning; untreated dirt makes the fabric rot.
  - Put new additions in a plastic bag with mothballs over night to kill any infestation.

Paw pads are usually made from felt and are especially prone to wear; this bear has replacement pads, which will affect its value.

Most bears are made from beige or gold mohair plush. Unusual colours are more desirable. Steiff also made some bears in red, black, apricot and white mohair.

AMERICAN BEARS

American bears, like this, were often unmarked but have distinctive wide barrel-shaped bodies, narrow arms and legs and small feet. Some have humps like German bears. £250+

Toys

If you are thinking of beginning a collection of toys there is a huge range of prices and varieties from which to choose. Many collectors specialize in a particular area, such as clockwork toys, robots or cars, or in a particular maker. You need to be sure of your area of interest before visiting the larger auction houses because many sell different types of toy – such as soldiers, model cars or trains – in specialist sales.

Prices for toys depend on the maker, the rarity of the model and the condition. Although chips and dents are virtually inevitable, a toy in mint condition, or with its original packaging is what every serious collector longs for. Repainting will nearly always reduce the value of a collector's toy so only repaint items in your collection as a last resort.

Toys made by well-known firms are always sought after, and minor damage is acceptable if the toy is made by a premium firm such as Bing, Märklin or Lehmann. Viewing sales and visiting specialist dealers is the best way of getting to know which models are the most desirable. Once you have a good feel for prices, you don't have to buy from an upmarket auction house or dealer. Because many collectable toys are not very old it's always worth scouring the local junk shop or jumble sale for bargains!

WOOD, LEAD &

Less sophisticated than toys made from other substances, carved wooden toys have an appealing naivety. Wooden toys were produced in quantity by German makers during the 18th and 19th centuries and some very collectable wooden toys were also made in America by the Schoenhut Co.

Lead became popular as a medium for various types of soldiers and other toys during the late 19th century. In Germany, France and England high quality solid and hollow-cast lead soldiers were produced by firms such as Lucotte, Heyde and William Britain and today these are among the most valuable of all toy soldiers.

Die-cast toys were also made by hollow casting and were first produced in France in c.1910. In England, Dinky Toys, part of the Meccano Co., dominated the market for die-cast toys from the 1930s-60s and rare Dinky advertising vans or unusual series are well worth looking out for.

DIE-CAST TOYS

Complete sets of die-cast toys are always desirable, especially when they come with their original packaging. Although this c.1937 box is battered it still doubles the value of the set of aeroplanes. £600-900

DIE-CAST TOYS

► WOODEN TOYS
Noah's Ark was a popular subject for German wooden toy-carvers. Value depends on size, quality and the number of animals; this 19th century one is large (69cm/27in wide), fairly elaborate and contains over 200 animals, so it would be worth £1,000–2,000; smaller, less elaborate arks cost from £200.

▼ VALUE
Many 20th century wooden toys are still affordably priced. This 1930s apple filled with skittles is worth £20-25.

▼ TOY SOLDIERS
Britain's are among the most sought after collector's soldiers and were made using the hollow-casting method. A hollow-cast figure will have a small hole where the excess molten metal was poured out of the mould when it was made. £2,500-3,500

TINPLATE, TRAINS & CELLULOID

Horse-drawn carriages, boats, submarines, cars and even airships are just some of the plethora of tinplate toys made during the late 19th and early 20th century which reflect contemporary developments in transport. German toy companies led the field in the manufacture of tinplate toys and those made by well-known firms such as Bing, Märklin and Lehmann are famed for their accuracy. Trains were one of the most important forms of transport from the mid-19th century and not surprisingly trains provided

▶ BING
This c.1906 Bing rear entry Tonneau with a clockwork mechanism is especially desirable because the high quality hand-enamelled paintwork is in near perfect condition. £5,000–8,000

◀ MÄRKLIN
Märklin toys, such as this spirit-fired torpedo boat, can be identified by their distinctive maker's mark, which in this case is stamped on the boat's rudder. £4,500–6,500

▲ TRAINS
The most valuable Märklin toys, made between 1895 and 1914, are nowadays well out of the price range of the average schoolboy. The company produced the first trains to use a numerical gauge system, to identify the differently-sized models available. This Gauge III engine, made c.1909, is the second largest size made and would be worth £20,000+.

toy makers with a fertile source of inspiration. The earliest toy trains were clockwork or made from wood but by c.1900 electric trains – the dream of every school boy ever since – began to be produced in substantial numbers.

Celluloid toys were made from the late 19th century. This substance became obsolete with the advent of plastics in the 20th century and nowadays celluloid toys are keenly collected although generally less expensive than tinplate toys of a similar date.

DISNEY TOYS

The earliest toys representing Disney characters were produced by German toy manufacturers such as Distler, who was probably responsible for this 1930s clockwork Mickey Mouse barrel organ toy. This thin, rather gloomy-looking Mickey is the most valuable. Even though he's lost his tail, Minnie has been repainted, and there are signs of rusting, the piece would still be worth over £1,500.

WHAT TO LOOK FOR

- Mickey and Minnie on a motorcycle, by Tipp & Co.
- Mickey the Musical Mouse, by Nifty
- Mickey the Drummer, by Nifty
- Donald Ducks with long bills.

◀ LICENSING
The box of this celluloid Mickey on Pluto, produced in Japan for the Western market, shows it's been made under special license and is therefore more desirable than an unauthorized version. £600

CELLULOID

Toys made from celluloid are highly flammable and prone to denting and cracking. The substance is almost impossible to restore satisfactorily, so avoid damaged celluloid toys.

Rock & Pop

Rock and pop memorabilia is one of the newest, most exciting and accessibly priced collecting areas – although it does have its high prices too – the record was $2.3 million paid for John Lennon's Rolls Royce in 1985.

Almost any object in some way connected with a well-known star can be collectable, so even tickets, posters and other printed ephemera made for concerts and tours are saleable. The most sought-after pieces are those closely linked with the stars themselves. Collectors pay especially high prices for the musical instruments with which a star is associated; electric guitars can fetch several thousands pounds if they were played at a memorable concert.

Clothes are another popular collecting area. The most valuable garments are those recognizably linked with the image of their owner. Perhaps they were photographed wearing them, or used them at an important concert, or in a video. Elton John's wacky shoes, Madonna's gold leather corset, Michael Jackson's rhinestone-studded glove have all attracted huge media attention and prices to match when they've come under the hammer. But not all collectable clothes are prohibitively expensive – prices for a roadie's jacket, or a T-Shirt sporting the name and logo of a tour or album start at less than £100.

THE 50S & 60S

The golden era of rock and roll is not surprisingly the focus for many collectors' attentions. Memorabilia from this period is relatively scarce compared with that of the following decades so even printed concert programmes and magazines, which were made in their thousands, and once cost only a few shillings, are keenly collected. The most desirable memorabilia relates to the big names of the period whose popularity endures today. Among the most popular are Elvis Presley, Buddy Holly, Bill Haley and Bob Dylan – to name but a few.

▲ **BUDDY HOLLY**
Buddy Holly continues to enjoy a keen following so memorabilia relating to his career attracts high prices. This signed souvenir programme marks his group's only tour to England. £850

▲ **JIM MORRISON**
Jim Morrison has always been collectable but his popularity enjoyed an upsurge with the release of Oliver Stone's film charting his life. These working lyrics for *The Celebration of the Lizard* give a revealing glimpse of Morrison's creative process and are worth £4,000-6,000.

BEATLES MEMORABILIA

The Beatles have a unique place in the history of pop music: no previous group had enjoyed such success and they pioneered the vibrant new pop music which epitomized the sounds of the 1960s. Although Beatles memorabilia comes up for sale quite regularly, almost any object which celebrates their fame is of interest to collectors.

▲ BEATLES DOLLS
The wide range of commercial Beatles merchandise made during the 1960s and 70s reflects the group's phenomenal popularity. Among the diverse Beatles objects which come up for sale are lamps, scrap books, wigs and stockings. These Beatles dolls, dressed in Sgt. Pepper's Lonely Hearts Club Band costumes, are worth £100–200.

▶ LENNON DRAWINGS
This hand-drawn Christmas card was given to Cynthia Powell by John Lennon in 1958 and encloses a revealing eight page letter to Cynthia, whom he married five years later. Drawings by John Lennon are among the most desirable pieces of Beatles memorabilia and can fetch very high prices. £8,800

▶ RINGO DRUM SET
Although this drum set is a toy it would attract collectors because it is rare to find these in near perfect condition, complete with stand, sticks, original box and instructions.
£250-400

WHAT TO LOOK FOR
● Hand written lyrics to famous songs
● Autographed and handwritten letters
● Autographed photographs
● Artwork for record sleeves
● Animation cells from *Yellow Submarine*

THE 70S

The 70s marked the heyday of rock star rebels such as The Sex Pistols, David Bowie, Marc Bolan and Bruce Springsteen whose new approach to rock music was to have a profound influence on musicians of the following generations. Because of its nostalgic appeal, memorabilia of the 70s is keenly collected, although pieces usually fetch less meteoric prices than the items which relate to the superstars of today.

▼ PETE TOWNSHEND
The fact that this guitar is smashed paradoxically adds to its value because it highlights its original owner's "bad boy" image. It's accompanied by a letter which details the guitar's history: *"… I broke it in 1973 in a rage of frustration in my studio…"*
£4,000–6,000

▲ THE ISLE OF WIGHT FESTIVAL
Posters relating to important concerts are among the most affordable pieces of rock and pop memorabilia. The pop festivals held in the Isle of Wight in 1969 and 1970 were key events and attracted audiences of over a quarter of a million. This promotional poster, from the 1970 concert is worth £50–70.

◄ ELTON JOHN
Elton John was one of the first stars to exploit the possibilities of stage costume. Extraordinary glasses and flamboyant shoes such as these became his trademark and are keenly collected. £300–600 (a pair)

THE 80S & 90S

The advent of the pop video was largely responsible for the increased importance stars of the 80s and 90s attached to their appearance and image. As concerts and tours became increasingly sophisticated, the star's visual impact became as important as the music. Costumes, often made by leading designers, are an obvious way of establishing the star's persona. Hence, outfits of increasingly extravagant design have become the symbol of many of the most famous celebrities of the past two decades.

▶ PRINCE

All Prince's clothes are specially made for him and because his swashbuckling outfits are fundamental to his on-stage image those that come up for sale are very desirable. This suit made from turquoise and blue silk was sold with a letter of authentication stating where it was made and confirming that it was worn at the 1988 Grammy Awards by Prince. £5,000+

TOP FIVE COLLECTABLE STARS

- **Michael Jackson** Leading light so almost anything is desirable.
- **Madonna** Changes her image for each tour so anything directly connected with one of her "looks" will be very desirable.
- **Prince** Neo-romantic clothes always sought after.
- **Elton John** Shoes, glasses, hats – the more zany the higher the price.
- **Queen** Anything connected with Freddy Mercury.

▲ MICHAEL JACKSON

Michael Jackson was often photographed wearing this rhinestone-studded glove which was perhaps the most instantly recognizable piece of Rock and Pop clothing of the decade. The glove sold in 1991 for £16,500; a record for any piece of Michael Jackson costume!

PRESENTATION DISCS

The most valuable awards are the gold and platinum discs presented by the record company to the star. Gold discs are given for over 500,000 albums, or 1 million singles sold; platinum discs are given for over 1 million albums or 2 million singles sold. This silver presentation disc for Madonna's *You Can Dance* is worth £200-350.

Whether because of their historical interest, high-quality craftsmanship, or because they are such potent reminders of the heroics of the past, the relics of war have long fascinated collectors. The terms "Arms and Militaria" cover a surprisingly wide range of objects and include armour, firearms, edged weapons, medals, badges, uniforms, and even prints and cigarette cards.

Armour has been made, in one form or another, from the dawn of civilization to the 19th century; but most pieces commonly seen on the market today date from the 16th century onwards. Full sets of armour are extremely valuable and if you're a novice collector you must learn to recognize the numerous "marriages" between pieces from different periods. So long as you realize the set is a composite and this fact is allowed for in the price, marriages are acceptable.

Antique firearms are often more accessibly priced. A 19th century flintlock pistol could cost £150 or less; 18th century examples are priced from about £300. Before you start buying, remember to check if a special licence is necessary. In most countries you don't need a licence to collect antique firearms, but you do if you intend firing them.

EDGED WEAPONS

Edged weapons, which include swords, sabres, dirks and bayonets, come up for sale frequently and, depending on the type of weapon you choose, it is possible to build up a collection for relatively little outlay. Most antique firearms fall into one of two categories: flintlocks, which use a flint to make a spark and ignite the charge; or percussion guns, in which a metal cap containing a small explosive charge is ignited by the stroke of the hammer. Even though most antique weapons are never used, the "feel" of a firearm is one of the most important factors to take into account when buying. Firearms should be well-balanced when you handle them. Pieces which feel top-heavy and uncomfortable in the firing position are less desirable.

◄ LONG ARMS
Unusual early weapons always command a premium. This German wheel-lock sporting rifle, dated 1666, has several quality features which make it particularly desirable:
- high quality engraving on the lock plate
- maker's mark
- elaborately inlaid stock decorated with stag horn, silver wire and mother-of-pearl. £3,000-5,000

SWORD CARE
- wipe blades clean after handling
- wax blades after cleaning
- clean rust spots by rubbing them with a copper coin.

& ANTIQUE FIREARMS

◄ DUELLING PISTOLS
In cased sets of pistols always check that all the pieces belong together and have not been added. This pair of American percussion duelling pistols comes with a range of accessories including Eley caps, and balls. £2,000–3,000

◄ SWORDS AND DIRKS
The less than perfect condition and evidence of honest wear you can see on this set of mid-19th century Scottish regimental swords are a good sign that the set is authentic. £3,500–5,500
● The small dagger in the centre is a Scottish dirk; these were carried by Scottish Highlanders.

BEWARE
● Fake engraving is sometimes added to swords to increase their value – be suspicious of harsh bright edges, and expect there to be signs of ageing, such as dirt and grease between the lines.
● When fake engraving is added to a piece which already has some decoration it will often be of a different depth from the original and the background colour will be different.

▼ DECORATION
The decoration on a sword reflects the status of its original owner and always adds to value. The blued and inlaid Napoleonic sabre (top) belonged to a high-ranking cavalry officer. The 1831 British general officer's sword (below) is less ornate. top £600–1,000, below £200–300

ARMOUR

Swashbuckling armour from the English Civil War period (1642-49) is still fought over, but nowadays by collectors! Favourite items include "lobster-tailed" helmets, pikeman's pots (simple helmets), breast and back plates and gauntlets. Because complete suits of original armour so rarely come up for sale, even good 19th century reproductions are highly collectable and valuable. Much good quality armour of this period was made in Germany, France and Spain.

▼ CONDITION

This three-quarter Armour dates from c.1640 and was made for a Cuirassier (horseman). It is in unusually fine condition and even has its original buckles. Most antique armour has been repaired at some stage. Modern repairs are usually gas welded and this leaves tell-tale burns on the surface.
£8,000-10,000

ARMOUR CARE
● Treat rust with equal quantities of turpentine and paraffin, and a little methylated spirit.
● Polish armour with balls of newspaper and protect with wax.

WHAT TO LOOK FOR
● Armourer's marks – add to value.
● Small dents in the breast plate – made from a pistol ball fired to test the armour's strength – a good sign of age.
● Funerary helmets – worn at funerals.

▲ REPRODUCTION ARMOUR

Although 19th century armour was intended for decorative rather than practical purposes, much of it was very well-made. The quality of this 16th century-style fluted Maximilian armour, made c.1820, is reflected in the thickness of the metal used. A good quality suit will weigh as much as 26-27kg (58-60lb).
£4,000-5,000

MISCELLANEOUS MILITARIA

The wide range of other collectable military antiques provides would-be collectors with huge scope. You may decide to concentrate on a particular regiment, a type of object, or on a period of military history. Complete early uniforms may be hard to find, but head-dresses, badges, fastenings, medals, powder flasks, postcards and prints are readily available and can form fascinating and highly decorative collections.

▶ BADGES

Whether made from metal or fabric badges are increasingly popular with collectors. Officer's head-dress badges are larger than most others and particularly sought after. British regimental badges such as these early 19th century examples are identifiable because they invariably include a crown in the design. £100-400 (each)

▶ MEDALS

Before buying a medal check the soldier's and regiment's history to make sure he was entitled to it. This rare group of medals, awarded to a Colonel in the Indian Army, is officially engraved with his name. £2,200-2,600

BEWARE

● Expect badges to show evidence of their age – those in perfect condition should make you suspicious.
● Fake badges usually weigh less than genuine ones and feel waxy.

▲ SHAKOS

Shakos, the cylindrical helmets, with peaks and often plumes, were popular during the 19th century. The elaborateness of their decoration can affect value. This Austro-Hungarian shako is reasonably ornate with plenty of gold trimming and is worth around £200.

SCIENTIFIC INSTRUMENTS

However tempting it is to imagine some famous scientist of the past making a dramatic discovery with your microscope, sadly this is usually a long way from the truth. Most early scientific instruments were made either for amateur scientists, who regarded them as objects of beauty, or for professionals such as surveyors, navigators, architects and even teachers, for whom these were everyday tools of their trade.

You don't have to be knowledgeable about the history of science to appreciate the obvious skill with which scientific instruments were made. At one end of the spectrum are the machine-made precision tools

◀ TELESCOPES
John Dollond perfected the use of achromatic lenses, which eliminated the problems of colour fringing (caused by the distortion of light) in telescopes. Instruments made by this leading 18th century London maker or his sons, Peter and John jnr, are usually signed *J.* or *P. Dollond London.* This one dates from the late 18th century and is worth £1,500–£2,000.

BEWARE
During the early l9th century unscrupulous dealers attempted to cash in on the Dollond reputation by selling telescopes falsely inscribed *Dolland.* These are still collectable but less valuable.

▶ SEXTANTS AND OCTANTS
Octants (so-called because their frame is one eighth of a circle) and sextants (one sixth of a circle) measure angular distance by means of reflective mirrors. Octants usually have wooden frames – mahogany, boxwood or ebony are typical. Sextants were usually brass-framed and more accurate than octants – and are often more expensive. This is an 18th century brass and ebony octant signed by J. MacDonald. £300+

produced during the 19th century, some of which can be bought for little over £100; at the other are the rare, expensive examples of 18th century (and earlier) hand-crafted objects. Many instruments are ornately decorated and incorporate materials such as brass, silver, ivory and ebony. The dating of a piece can present inexperienced collectors with a problem, as the same design was often repeated over long periods. Some instruments were marked by their maker, and this usually helps with identification and dating, but also will usually increase the price. Fakes and reproductions of early instruments exist, so if in doubt always consult an expert.

NEVER ... attempt to polish an old scientific instrument of any type without checking with an expert first, if you do so you may seriously damage its patina, and reduce its value dramatically.

▲ GLOBES
Terrestrial pocket globes reflect advances in mapping and circumnavigation of the world and often had cases lined with celestial globes – maps of the stars. This one was made by J. Smith in 1815. £1,700-2,000

◀ SUNDIALS
Before watches became widely accessible and reliable, dials were often used to check the time. There are two main types of sundial: the pedestal dial, most commonly used in the garden, and the pocket dial. This typical 18th century octagonal pocket dial has an elaborately decorated brass plate and a folding gnomon (the part that casts the shadow). £300-400

▼ MICROSCOPES
This Culpeper-type microscope dates from c.1730 and is one of the most desirable types of early microscope (worth £4,000-6,000). Microscopes from the 19th century are easier to find. Names to look out for are: Powell & Lealand, W & S Jones, James Powell Swift, Smith & Beck.

CAMERAS & PHOTOGRAPHS

Although old cameras seem worlds apart from the high-tech models of today, many are still in working order and are bought to use. The earliest commercially-made cameras were produced from c.1841 and used the daguerreotype process, developed in France by L. J. M. Daguerre, in 1837. However, each daguerreotype image was unique and it was not until Henry Fox Talbot's invention of the calotype that multi-copies could be produced from a single exposure. Among the most intriguing of cameras are the novelty, detective and spy cameras which began to be produced as the photographic process became more refined towards the end of the century.

Unlike many other collectables, a camera's age is not necessarily reflected in its value – the rarity and quality of a particular model are often far more important than when it was made. Japanese cameras, which have enjoyed an upsurge in popularity recently, were mass produced in the aftermath of World War II. Their quality became widely appreciated as a result of photojournalists covering the Korean War who recognized the superior quality of Japanese lenses. Today, rare and limited edition models by companies such as Nikon or Canon can fetch very high prices.

▶ **DAGUERREOTYPES**
Daguerreotypes look like mirrors – the image is formed on silvered metal, usually protected behind sealed glass. Despite their relative rarity you can still find portrait groups such as this for £30–40. An interesting view or a known sitter adds to value, which can be £1,000 or more.

◀ **PHOTOGRAPH ALBUMS**
The value of early albums is affected by the subject matter of the photos and the quality of the album. This one is made from leather and mother-of-pearl. Some were made from ivory, silver, gold or mauchline ware – wood covered with tartan-printed paper. £50–80

WHAT TO LOOK FOR

- milestone cameras which incorporate unusual technical innovations
- early handmade brass and mahogany cameras
- unusual spy cameras
- rare models by Ernst Leitz (Leica) and Zeiss
- limited edition post World War II Japanese cameras.

▶ DETECTIVE AND SPY CAMERAS

Cameras in the form of books, watches, rings and packets of cigarettes may have been made more as curiosities than for any real espionage or skulduggery, but are none the less highly popular with today's collectors – and can fetch very high prices. This c.1895 camera looks just like a pocket watch when closed and measures only 4cm (1¾in)

diameter. Made by an American maker, John C. Hegelein, it's worth £15,000–25,000.

▲ BRASS AND MAHOGANY CAMERAS

Early mahogany and brass-bound cameras are always sought after, but this 1890 Cyclographe is especially rare because it is the first panoramic camera produced by the prominent French maker V. Damoizeau. A clockwork mechanism rotated the camera around the platform and wound on the film automatically. £8,000–£12,000

▶ JAPANESE CAMERAS

The quality and condition of post-war cameras has an important bearing on their price. Because this Nikon S3M is one of only 195 models made in the series, and is in nearly mint condition, it would be worth over £12,000. A similar used model would be worth about £6,000.

FILM MEMORABILIA

Although there's nothing new about the magnetic allure of the cinema, film memorabilia is one of the most recent and exciting arrivals on the collecting scene. All the glamour of the movies, from the nostalgic old films of Hollywood's golden age, to the high-tech special effect films of the 1980s and 90s, are reflected in the objects which fall into this colourful collecting category.

The major types of collectable film memorabilia are costumes, props, autographs, posters and photographs; but almost anything associated with a particular film or star can be collectable. Props associated with the key stars of cult movies tend to attract the highest prices. If a particular object immediately conjures up an important star you're on to a winner – but you'll probably have to pay for it! If you can't afford the thousands needed to buy objects such as Charlie Chaplin's bowler hat and cane, or Harrison Ford's whip, you can still join in the fun by collecting the more affordable types of film memorabilia available. Posters, photographs, autographs and clapperboards, are often priced at less than £100.

▶ **PHOTOGRAPHS**
This portrait photograph of Marlene Dietrich dates from c.1935, but even recently reproduced photos are desirable, because to many collectors the image of the star is more important than the age of the photograph. £300–550

BEWARE
Autographs on photos are often not genuine:
● Many stars allowed their secretaries to sign photographs on their behalf.
● Sometimes the negative of the photograph was signed.
● Some photographs are stamped with the star's signature.

◀ **POSTERS**
Among the most desirable film posters are those from classic films of the 50s and 60s. *Breakfast at Tiffany's* met with enormous success when it was released in 1961, and firmly established Audrey Hepburn as a star of the first order. This poster fetched £400. Posters for lesser films cost under £10.

◀ PROPS
This gruesome head was used in *Aliens 3* for close-up sequences of Charles Dance, who played Superintendent Clemens in the 1992 film. Its high value is a reflection of three key points:

- rarity – it was the only one made
- the character was a key one in the film
- *Alien* films were hugely popular. £2,000

▼ THUNDERBIRDS
The demand for Thunderbirds memorabilia has been fuelled by the recent re-screening of the series on TV. Even though this is only a replica of Thunderbird 3, and wasn't used in filming, it's still worth £600-800.

▲ STAR WARS
The best film props are surprisingly well made and sophisticated. Darth Vadar's helmet is made from fibreglass and has see-through perspex panels inserted in the cheek and neck areas to give better visibility to the wearer during the fighting sequences of *Star Wars*. £3000+

▶ CLAPPERBOARDS
Clapperboards are among the least expensive types of film memorabilia. Look for boards which come from popular films, and which are printed with the name of the production. £40+

SPORTING COLLECTABLES

If your attic is filled with mouldering old golf clubs you may be astonished to know that a club recently fetched £92,400 at auction! While such a staggering price is very much the exception, there are, nonetheless, increasing numbers of sportsmen who bring their passion for field, pitch, or river bank into their homes by collecting objects related to their favoured pastime. Prices have also been boosted by the fashion for traditional decor which has inspired many an interior designer to furnish elegant hallways and studies with the paraphernalia of time-honoured sport.

In the not too distant past old sporting equipment was usually relegated to the junk shop; nowadays you're more likely to find it in upmarket auction houses, and there are also a number of dealers who specialize in this field.

The most sought after sporting items relate to the most popular pastimes: hence golf, fishing, football, tennis, cricket, rugby, and even skiing memorabilia are keenly collected by enthusiasts. Collectable items include not only the objects needed to pursue the sport – whether rods, reels, golf clubs, balls or rackets – but also trophies of the sport and ceramic and printed ephemera relating to it.

◀ **GOLF**
Pre-19th century golfing collectables are extremely rare, which explains why this late 17th–early 18th century club made by a blacksmith reached a world record price of £92,400 when it was sold at auction last year.

WHAT TO LOOK FOR
- Clubs marked by one of the great makers such as Auchterlonie, Andrew Forgan, Jack Morris or Philp.
- Feathery golf balls – made from hand stitched leather stuffed with dampened goose down.
- Pottery commemorating golfing events or personalities, especially if made by premier factories such as Spode and Doulton.

▲ **19TH CENTURY CLUBS**
Early clubs had names rather than numbers. These are drivers, and long-nosed spoons of varying sizes. Price depends on rarity, age, quality and condition. Wood and iron clubs were made until the l930s and can be bought for as little as £20-30. These all date from c.1885 and vary in price from £1,500-3,500.

◄ **FISHING**
Perhaps as a substitute for "the one that got away", fishing trophies of the late 19th-early 20th century have lured many a collector in recent years. The most desirable fish are those in bow-fronted cases, such as this, which contains a bream caught in 1935. £700-900

▲ **FISHING TACKLE**
Early reels were finely made from materials such as brass, ivorene and ebonite (simulated ebony); marked ones are particularly desirable. Among the names to look out for are Hardy Bros of Alnwick, Charles Farlow, S. Allcock and Alfred Illingworth. These reels all date from the late 19th and early 20th century and are worth between £150 (top right) to £2,000 (bottom right).

CONDITION
Reels in mint condition are rare, but those with damaged or replaced parts, or their owner's name scratched on them (unless he's famous) are best avoided.

▼ **TENNIS**
Even if he or she never won a match with it, a famous owner can transform even a modern racket into a valuable collector's item; but provenance is all-important. This Wilson racket is autographed by Jimmy Connors; who used it in the 1979-81 US Opens, and comes with a letter of authenticity. £1,500-2,000

BOXES

Boxes come in a huge range of shapes, sizes and prices; some of the most exquisite ones were produced during the 18th century to contain snuff, patches or tobacco. The highest quality boxes were often made from gold or silver, perhaps decorated with precious stones. Enamelled and porcelain boxes were also popular, some of the most attractive being made in the shape of a bird or animal. Although small 18th century boxes can easily cost £1,000 or more, you can still find attractive 19th century versions for much less. Price is usually determined by quality and materials used. In general, boxes made from wood or *papier mâché* are widely available and most affordable.

▲ LACQUER BOXES
Lids of 19th century lacquer boxes were often decorated with a copy of a well-known Old Master – erotic subjects were always especially popular. This one shows nymphs bathing, with mischievous voyeurs in the bulrushes! Like many boxes of this type it was made in Germany, and is stamped on the interior *Stobwasser Fabrik*. £300–500

▼ ENAMEL BOXES
Bilston (Staffordshire), Birmingham and Battersea led the field in producing English enamel boxes during the 18th century. Chipping will reduce value; this late 18th century box is damaged around the base and is worth about £80; in better condition it might cost twice as much.

▲ TORTOISESHELL BOXES
Tortoiseshell, moulded by heat and pressure, was often used for making small boxes during the 18th and 19th centuries. This 19th century cigar case is decorated with stellar *piqué*, (an inlay of gold or silver). £200–300

◄ TUNBRIDGE WARE
Tunbridgeware decoration was mostly made, as the name suggests, in the Tunbridge Wells area of Kent. This fiddly technique involved making pictures from long strands of differently coloured woods which were glued together, and sliced transversally into thin sheets. Value depends on the fineness of the decoration; this one is of average quality. £300–500

VINTAGE FOUNTAIN PENS

Condition is a prime factor in the value of old pens, as they can be expensive to restore, so check carefully for signs of excessive wear. Avoid pens with replacement parts, which have often been forced or glued to the body. Pens in excellent condition are worth four or five times as much as worn ones.

PREMIER PENS

Quality pens (before 1945) by these makers are especially desirable: Parker (before 1930) ● Waterman ● Montblanc ● Mabie Todd Co. (Swan) ● Wahl-Eversharp ● Sheaffer ● Dunhill-Namiki.

---

1 Pens marked as a calendar with dates and the seven days of the week were only made by Waterman. This was made in 1936 from 9ct gold. £800–1,000

2 The crescent on the side of this c.1916 gold-plated Conklin was a new design patented by this US maker in 1899 to improve the way the pen was filled. £300–500

3 This c.1905 silver Swan eyedropper is especially valuable because of its high quality scroll and lozenge decoration. £300–500

4 It probably took as long as 2 weeks to decorate this c.1935 Dunhill-Namiki pen with such high-quality lacquer decoration. £1,500+

5 The Lily pattern decorating this pen is one of the rarest designs used by Swan during the early years of the 20th century. £1,200

6 This Montblanc pen, made c.1924, is of a fairly standard design, but is still worth £800–1,200, because the case is decorated with gold overlay.

7 Although this gold-plated Conklin filigree pen made c.1918 is a more common type than No. 2, it's in a larger size so would still be worth £300–500.

8 There are fakes of this unusual "spider's web" c.1924 Montblanc Model 1M but they are usually suspiciously "new" in appearance. £1,000–2,000

9 This "Smallest pen in the World" was a novelty made by Waterman c.1910–15; one was made for Queen Mary's Dolls House. £1,200+

● Waterman also produced a massive No. 20 safety pen – these were reputedly used in America for hiding Whisky during the Prohibition!

TRIBAL ART

The strong images and primitive shapes which characterize tribal art have enjoyed a huge increase in popularity in recent years. However, because prices have risen steeply and the demand for genuine old pieces has greatly outstripped supply, there has also been a huge increase in fake pieces on the market. The many fakes produced in Africa and the Far East for the tourist market can be very hard to identify, so if you're an inex-perienced collector, buy from a reputable source who can guarantee the age of any piece purporting to be old.

Provenance is fundamental to the value of tribal art. The most desirable pieces are those which have at some time been used for their intended domestic, ceremonial or ritual purpose, and were perhaps collected by colonial settlers or missionaries during the 19th or early 20th century.

WHAT TO LOOK FOR

- Clubs from the Pacific Islands – smaller ones were thrown at enemies to knock them over, larger ones for killing them!
- Weapons with figurative carving.
- Silver African tribal jewellery.
- Benin bronzes – often faked, so beware.
- Baule masks from the Ivory Coast.

◀ MASKS
Masks are one of the most popular collecting areas of tribal art; many were used in tribal festivities and have symbolic significance. This Sepik mask is particularly valuable because of its provenance: it comes from the collection of Frank Wonder who acquired it on an expedition to New Guinea in the 1920s. £5,000–7,000

◀ CONDITION
Because of the extremes of the African climate, wooden objects which predate the early 20th century are rare. Wooden objects often deteriorate, but a worn patina, as seen on this Urhobo male figure, is a desirable feature and adds to value. £3,000–4,000

▶ CALABASHES
The Hawaiian Calabash bowl, was a status symbol made from the finest quality woods, and passed down through families. Before the early 19th century they were usually hand-carved, later examples were made on a lathe. Because the elaborate butterfly repairs on this one enhance its aesthetic appeal, it's worth £4,000.

ANTIQUITIES

If, like many collectors, you've always assumed that antiquities are prohibitively expensive, you may be surprised to find out that the average auction of antiquities contains many objects priced at hundreds rather than thousands of pounds. Nonetheless, antiquities have long been sought after, and faking in one form or another has existed throughout the centuries. There is also the added complication of export laws which exist in most countries where antiquities originate. Collectors should always make sure the piece is being sold legally.

BEWARE
- Antiquities are fragile and condition affects value, but some damage is to be expected – be suspicious of anything which seems too perfect.
- Avoid objects with heavy restoration – particularly if it is on the face of a piece of sculpture or a painting.
- Avoid bronzes which have become badly corroded – their detail may have been irreparably damaged.

▲ EGYPTIAN ANTIQUITIES
Egyptian antiquities can be extremely valuable but there are exceptions. This red-ware vase dates from 3,500–3,200BC and is worth about £200. Other inexpensive antiquities include:
- small Egyptian limestone carvings
- roman terracotta oil lamps
- small examples of Cypriot pottery.

▼ ROMAN GLASS
It might seem inconceivable that glass from the 2nd century can be no more expensive than that of the 18th century, but this is often the case. These vases illustrate the subtle colours and iridescence typical of much Roman glass and are worth between £300–800 each.

REMEMBER...
If you have any doubts about the legality or authenticity of a piece consult museum experts.

◀ GREEK POTTERY
Valuable Greek pottery is often decorated with scenes from mythology. This Attic (made in Athens) black-figure amphora (two-handled urn) dates from c.510–500BC, and shows Peleus chasing Thetis. Attic vases with reversed colours (background black and figures red) are known as red-figure vases. £8,000–12,000

PART 4

FACT FILE

ABOVE A SELECTION OF INVALUABLE
COLLECTOR'S GUIDES.

LEFT RECORDING PRICES AT BERMONDSEY
ANTIQUES MARKET.

WHERE TO SEE

There is an abundance of places where you can see and study antiques. Some of the major collections to be found in museums and houses open to the public are listed below.

American Museum in Britain
Claverton Manor,
Bath, Avon
Ceramics, Clocks, Furniture, Silver

Aspley House
Wellington Museum,
149 Piccadilly, Hyde
Park Corner,
London W1
Ceramics, Militaria

Ashmolean Museum
Beaumont Street,
Oxford
Ceramics, Clocks, Glass, Silver

Attingham Park
Shrewsbury,
Shropshire
Furniture, Silver

Belton House
Grantham, Lincs
Ceramics, Furniture, Silver, Textiles

Bethnal Green Museum of Childhood
Cambridge Heath
Road,
London E2
Dolls, Toys

Birmingham Art Gallery

Chamberlain Square,
Birmingham
Glass

Blenheim Palace
Woodstock, Oxon
Furniture, Silver, Glass, Ceramics

Blickling Hall
Blickling,
Norwich,
Norfolk
Furniture, Textiles

Bristol City Art Gallery
Queen's Road,
Bristol
Glass

British Museum
Great Russell Street,
London WC1
Antiquities, Ceramics, Clocks, Glass, Silver

Burghley House
Stamford, Northants
Furniture

The Burrel Collection,
Pollock Country
Park, Glasgow
Antiquities, Decorative Arts, Oriental Art

Castle Museum
Nottingham
Ceramics

Castle Museum
Tower Street,
York
Ceramics, Silver, Sheffield Plate

Cecil Higgins Art Gallery and Museum
Castle Close,
Bedford
Ceramics, Glass

Clandon Park
West Clandon,
Guildford
Ceramics, Furniture, Textiles

Cutler's Company
Hallamshire,
Cutler's Hall,
Church Street,
Sheffield
Silver, Sheffield Plate

Derby Museum & Art Gallery
The Strand,
Derby
Porcelain

Dyson Perrins Museum
Seven Street,
Worcester
Ceramics

Felbrigg Hall
Norwich,
Norfolk
Furniture

Fenton House
Windmill Hill,
Hampstead,
London NW3

Ceramics, Furniture

Fitzwilliam Museum
Trumpington Street,
Cambridge
Ceramics, Clocks, Glass

Geffrye Museum
Kingsland Road,
London E2
Furniture, Decorative Arts

Glasgow Art Gallery & Museum
Kelvingrove,
Glasgow
Ceramics, silver

Greyfriars
Friar Street,
Worcester
Furniture, Textiles

Gunby Hall
Gunby,
Near Spilsby,
Lincolnshire
Furniture

Ham House
Richmond,
Surrey
Furniture

Hampton Court Palace
Hampton, Middlesex
Ceramics, Furniture, Rugs, Textiles

Harewood House
Leeds, West
Yorkshire
Furniture

Ickworth
Ickworth,
The Rotunda,
Horringer,
Bury St Edmunds
Furniture, Silver

**Imperial War
Museum**
Lambeth Road,
London SE1
Arms and Armour

Knole
Sevenoaks, Kent
*Carpets, Ceramics,
Furniture, Textiles*

**Laing Art Gallery
and Museum**
Higham Place,
Newcastle
Ceramics, Glass

**Lady Lever Art
Gallery**
Port Sunlight, Wirral,
Merseyside
Furniture

Longleat House
Warminster, Wilts
Ceramics, Furniture

**Manchester City
Art Gallery**
Mosley Street,
Manchester
Glass

Montacute House
Montacute,
Somerset
Furniture, Textiles

**National Maritime
Museum**

Romney Road,
Greenwich,
London SE10
*Scientific and
Navigational
Instruments*

**National Museum
of Ireland**
Kildare Street and
Marrion Street,
Dublin
Glass

Petworth House
Petworth, Sussex
Furniture, Sculpture

**Pilkington Glass
Museum**
Pilkington Brothers
Ltd., Prescot Road,
St Helens,
Merseyside
Glass

Osterley Park
Isleworth,
Middlesex
Ceramics, Furniture

Polesden Lacey
Dorking,
Surrey
*Ceramics, Furniture,
Photograph, Silver*

**Royal Museum of
Scotland**
Chambers Street,
Edinburgh
Decorative Arts

Royal Pavilion
Brighton,
Sussex

*Ceramics, Furniture,
Glass, Rugs, Textiles*

Rufford Old Hall
Rufford,
Ormskirk,
Lancashire
*Armour, Arms,
Furniture, Textiles*

**The Science
Museum**
Exhibition Road,
London SW7
*Barometers, Scientific
Instruments*

**Sheffield City
Museum,**
Weston Park,
Sheffield
Sheffield Plate

Shugborough
Milford,
Near Stafford,
Staffordshire
*Ceramics, Furniture,
Silver*

Standen
East Grinstead,
Sussex
*Art Nouveau Ceramics,
Furniture, Textiles*

**Stoke-on-Trent
City Museum and
Art Gallery**
Broad Street,
Hanley, Stoke-on-
Trent
Ceramics

Syon House
Brentford, Middlesex
Clocks

Tatton Park
Knutsford,
Cheshire
*China, Furniture,
Glass, Silver*

**Temple Newsam
House,**
Leeds
*Ceramics, Furniture,
Silver*

**Victoria and Albert
Museum**
Cromwell Road,
London SWl
*Art Nouveau,
Ceramics, Clocks,
Furniture, Glass, Rugs
and Carpets, Silver,
Textiles*

Waddesdon Manor
Aylesbury, Bucks.
*Carpets, Ceramics,
Furniture*

Wallace Collection
Hertford House,
Manchester Square,
London W1
Ceramics, Furniture

Windsor Castle
Windsor, Berkshire
*Ceramics, Clocks,
Furniture, Rugs*

WHERE TO BUY

MAJOR AUCTION HOUSES

Bearnes
Rainbow,
Avenue Road,
Torquay,
Devon
Tel 0803 296277

Bonhams
Montpelier Street,
London SW7
Tel 071 584 9161

Christie's Manson & Woods Ltd.
8 King Street,
St James's,
London SW1
Tel 071 839 9060

Henry Spencer & Son
20 The Square,
Retford,
Notts.
Tel 0777 708633

Lawrences of Crewkerne
South Street,
Crewkerne,
Somerset
Tel 0460 73041

Lots Road Auction Galleries
71 Lots Road,
London SW10
Tel 071 351 7771

Outhwaite & Litherland
Kingsway Galleries,
Fontenoy Street,
Liverpool
Tel 051 236 6561

Phillips
Blenstock House,
101 New Bond Street,
London W1
Tel 071 629 6602

Rosebery's
The Old Railway
Booking Hall,
Crystal Palace Station
Road,
London SE19
Tel 081 778 4024

Sotheby's
34–35 New Bond
Street,
London W1
Tel 071 493 8080

MAJOR ANTIQUES FAIRS

JANUARY

London Ceramics Fair
*Cumberland Hotel
Marble Arch,
London W1
Tel 0634 723461*

West London Antiques Fair
Town Hall,
Hornton Street,
London W8
Tel 0444 483514

The LAPADA Antiques and Fine Art Fair
National Exhibition
Centre,
Birmingham
Tel 021 780 4141

FEBRUARY

Harrogate Antique and Fine Art Fair
The Royal Baths,
Harrogate, Yorks
Tel 0823 323363

London Antique Dealers' Fair
Café Royal,

Regent Street,
London W1
Tel 0672 870727

MARCH

Kenilworth Antique Fair
Chesford Grange,
Kenilworth
Tel 0672 870727

The Chelsea Antiques Fair
Chelsea Old Town
Hall,
King's Road,
London SW3
Tel 0444 483514

Cheshire County Antiques Fair
Arley Hall,
Near Knutsford,
Cheshire
Tel 0672 515558

The Decorative Antiques and Textiles Fair
Chelsea Harbour,
The Marquee,
Lots Road,
London SW10
Tel 071 624 5173

Wilton House Antiques Fair
Wilton House,
Wilton,
Near Salisbury,
Wiltshire
Tel 0722 743115

APRIL

The British International Antiques Fair
National Exhibition
Centre,
Birmingham
Tel 021 780 4141

TVADA Antiques Fair,
School Hall,
Eton,
Windsor,
Berks
Tel 0491 34393

MAY

The British Antique Dealers Association Fair
The Duke of York's
Headquarters,
Chelsea,
London SW3
Tel 0892 547590

Buxton Antiques Fair
The Pavilion
Gardens,
Buxton,
Derbyshire
Tel 0483 422562

JUNE

The Fine Art and Antiques Fair
Olympia,
London SW5
Tel 071 370 8211

Grosvenor House Antiques Fair
Grosvenor House
Hotel,
Park Lane,
London W1
Tel 071 499 6363

The International Ceramics Fair
The Park Lane Hotel,
Piccadilly,
London W1
Tel 071 734 5491

Westminster Antiques Fair
Royal Horticultural

Society's Old Hall,
Vincent Square,
London SW1
Tel 0444 483514

AUGUST
**West London
Antiques Fair**
Kensington Town
Hall,
Hornton Street,
London W8
Tel 0444 483514

SEPTEMBER
**The Decorative
Antiques and
Textiles Fair**
Chelsea Harbour,
The Marquee,
Lots Road,
London SW10
Tel 071 624 5173
**The Northern
Antiques Fair**
The Assembly
Rooms,
Harrogate,
Yorkshire
Tel 0223 832852

OCTOBER
**The Park Lane
Antiques Fair**
Park Lane Hotel,
Piccadilly,
London W1
Tel 071 371 1703

NOVEMBER
**Kensington
Antiques Fair**
Kensington Town
Hall,
Hornton Street,
London W8
Tel 0483 422562

**The International
Art and Antiques
Fair**
Harrods,
Knightsbridge,
London SW1
Tel 071 734 5491

DECEMBER
**City Fine Art and
Antiques Fair,**
Barbican,
Golden Lane,
London EC4
Tel 081 660 8008
**Westminster
Antiques Fair**
Royal Horticultural
Society's Old Hall,
Vincent Square,
London SW1
Tel 0444 483514
Orangerie Italiana
24 Rutland Gate,
London SW7
Tel 071 225 3474

**ANTIQUES
MARKETS &
CENTRES**
**Alfie's Antiques
Market**
13-25 Church Street,
London W1
Tel 071 723 6066
(Tuesday-Saturday)
Antiquarius
King's Road,
Chelsea,
London SW3
Tel 071 351 5353
(Monday- Saturday)
**Bath Antique
Market**
Guinea Lane,
Landsdown Road,
Bath, Avon

Tel 071 351 5353
(Wednesdays)
**Bermondsey
Market**
Bermondsey Street,
London SE1
(Friday from 5 a.m.)
Camden Passage
Islington,
London N1
Tel 071 354 2839
(Tuesday-Saturday)
Chenil Galleries
King's Road,
Chelsea,
London SW3
Tel 071 351 5353
(Monday-Saturday)
**Cloisters Antique
Fairs**
St Andrews Hall,
Norwich,
Norfolk
Tel 0603 425158
(Wednedays)
**Gray's Antique
Market**
Davies Street,
London W1
Tel 071 629 7034
(Monday – Friday)
**Great Western
Antique Centre**
Bartlett Street,
Bath, Avon
Tel 0225 424243
**Portobello Road
Antiques Market**
Portobello Road,
London W11
(Saturdays)
**Preston Antique
Centre**
The Mill,
New Hall Lane,
Preston,
Lancashire

Tel 0772 794498
(Monday-Sunday)
**Taunton Silver
Street Antiques
Centre**
27-29 Silver Street,
Taunton,
Somerset
071 351 5353
(Mondays)
The Antique Centre
56 Garstang Road,
Preston,
Lancashire
Tel 0772 882078
(Monday – Sunday)
The Lanes
Brighton,
East Sussex
(Monday-Saturday)
**Woburn Abbey
Antiques Centre**
Woburn Abbey,
Woburn,
Bedfordshire
Tel 052529 0350
(Monday – Sunday)

**ANTIQUES
DEALERS'
ASSOCIATIONS**
**British Antiques
Dealers'
Association
(BADA)**
20 Rutland Gate
London SW7 1BD
Tel 071 589 4128
**London and
Provincial Antique
Dealers'
Association**
Suite 214,
535 Kings Road,
London SW10 0SZ
Tel 071 823 3511

WHAT TO READ

General

Bly, John *Is it Genuine?* (1986)

Collins, *Encyclopedia of Antiques* (1973)

Fleming, John, and Honour, Hugh, *The Penguin Dictionary of the Decorative Arts* (1977)

Hughes, Therle, *The Country Life Antiques Handbook* (1986)

Miller, Martin and Judith, *Miller's Antiques Price Guide* (1992)

Miller's Pocket Antiques Fact File (1988)

Miller's Pocket Dictionary of Antiques (1990)

Miller's Understanding Antiques (1989)

Osborne, Harold, *The Oxford Companion to the Decorative Arts* (1985)

Savage, George, *Dictionary of Antiques* (1970)

Simpson, M., and Huntley, M. (Ed.), *Sotheby's Caring for Antiques* (1992)

Furniture

Aguis, Pauline, *British Furniture 1880-1915* (1978)

Aslin, Elizabeth, *Nineteenth Century English Furniture*

(1962)

Bly, John, *Discovering English Furniture* (1976)

Chinnery, Victor, *Oak Furniture – The British Tradition* (1979)

Collard, Frances, *Regency Furniture* (1983)

Comstock, Helen, *Victorian Furniture and Windsor Chairs* (1958)

Edwards, R., *Shorter Dictionary of English Furniture* (1964)

Edwards, R., and M. Jourdain, *Georgian Cabinet-Makers* (1955)

Hayward, Helena, *World Furniture* (1965)

Jervis, Simon, *Victorian Furniture* (1968)

Joy, Edward, T., *English Furniture 1800-1851* (1977)

Miller, Martin and Judith, *Miller's Antiques Checklist – Furniture* (1991)

Payne, Christopher, *19th Century European Furniture* (1985)

(Ed.) *Sotheby's Concise Encyclopedia of Furniture* (1989)

Symonds, W.R. and B.B. Whinneray, *Victorian Furniture* (1978)

Ceramics

Atterbury, Paul, *History of Porcelain* (1982)

Battie, David and Michael, Turner, *The Price Guide to 19th & 20th Century Pottery*

Charleston, Robert Ed., *World Ceramics* (1981)

Godden, G.A. *Eighteeenth Century English Porcelain,* (1985)

Encyclopedia of British Pottery & Porcelain Manufacturers (1988)

Illustrated Encyclopedia of British Pottery and Porcelain

Oriental Export Market Porcelains (1979)

Staffordshire Porcelain (1983)

Halfpenny, Pat, *English Earthenware Figures 1740-1840* (1992)

Hillier, Bevis, *Pottery and Porcelain 1700-1914* (1968)

Honey, W.B., *French Porcelain of the 18th Century* (1950)

Hughes, Bernard and Therle, *English Porcelain and Bone China, 1743-1850* (1955)

Jenyns, Soame, *Japanese Porcelain* (1985)

Medley, Margaret, *The Art of the Chinese Potter* (1981)

Morley-Fletcher, Hugo, *Meissen* (1971)

Oliver, Anthony, *Staffordshire Pottery – The Tribal Art of England* (1981)

Savage, George, *Porcelain through the Ages* (1954)

Saville, Rosalind, *Sèvres Porcelain* (1980)

Sato, M., *Chinese Ceramics, A Short History,* (1981)

Sotheby's, *Concise Encylopedia of Porcelain* (1990)

Thomas, E. Lloyd, *Victorian Pottery* (1974)

Williams-Wood, Cyril, *Staffordshire Pot Lids and their Potters* (1972)

Glass

Bickerton, L., *18th Century English Drinking Glasses* (1986)

Dodsworth, Roger, *Glass and Glassmakers* (1982)

Grover, Ray and Lee, *Art Nouveau Glass* (1967)

Hajdamach, C., *British & European 19th Century Glass*

Mackay, James, *Glass Paperweights* (1973)

O'Looney, Betty, *Victorian Glass* (1972)

Slack, R., *English
Pressed Glass* (1987)
*Sotheby's Concise
Encyclopedia of
Glass* (1991)
Wakefield, Hugh,
*Nineteenth Century
British Glass* (1961)

Silver & Gold

Bradbury, Frederick,
*Bradbury's Book of
Hallmarks* (1975)
*History of Old Sheffield
Plate* (1968)
Brett, Vanessa,
*Sotheby's Directory
of Silver* (1986)
Bury, Shirley,
Victorian Electroplate
(1971)
Clayton, Michael,
*The Collector's
Dictionary of Gold
and Silver* (1985)
Culme, J., *Directory of
Gold & Silversmiths
1838-1914* (1987)
Grimwade, Arthur,
*London Goldsmiths
1697-1837* (1976)
Hughes, G., Bernard,
*Small Antique
Silverware (including
flatware)* (1971)
Jackson, Charles,
*English Goldsmiths
and Their Marks*
(1921)
Pickford I., *Silver
Flatware*
*Sotheby's Concise
Encyclopedia of
Silver* (1991)
Waldron, Peter, *Price
Guide to Antique
Silver*(1982)

Carpets & Textiles

Bennett, Ian, *Rugs
and Carpets of the
World* (1977)
Black, David (Ed.)
*World Rugs and
Carpets* (1985)
Edwards, A. Cecil,
The Persian Carpet
(1953)
Eiland, Murray,
*Oriental Rugs, A
Comprehensive
Guide* (1976)
Ford, P.R.J., *Oriental
Carpet Design*
Franses, Jack,
*European and
Oriental Rugs* (1970)
Godden, G. A.,
*Stevengraphs and
other Victorian Silk
Pictures* (1971)
Hughes, Therle,
*English Domestic
Needlework* (1961)

Clocks

Bird, A., *English
House Clocks 1600-
1850* (1973)
Britten, F. J., *Britten's
Watch and
Clockmakers
Handbook* (1982)
Bruton, Eric, *Antique
Clocks and Clock
Collecting* (1974)
Cescinsky, Herbert,
and Webster,
Malcolm R.,
*English Domestic
Clocks* (1976)
Loomes, Brian, *Early
Clockmakers of
Great Britain* (1981)
Miller Martin and

Judith (Ed.),
*Miller's Antiques
Checklist – Clocks*
(1992)

Art Nouveau/ Art Deco

Arwas, Victor, *Art
Deco* (1980)
*Dawes, Nicholas, M.,
Lalique Glass* (1986)
Garner, Philippe
(Ed.), *Phaidon
Encyclopedia of
Decorative Arts
1890-1940* (1978)
Hillier, Bevis, *Posters*
(1969)
The World of Art Deco
(1971)
Miller, Martin and
Judith, *Miller's
Antiques Checklist –
Art Deco* (1991)
*Miller's Antiques
Checklist – Art
Nouveau* (1992)

Bears Dolls & Toys

Ayres, W. S., *The
Main Street Pocket
Guide to Toys* (1981)
Brewster, K., and
Waugh, R., *The
Official Price Guide
to Antique and
Modern Teddy Bears*
(1988)
Coleman, E. A. D.,
and E. J., *The
Collector's
Encyclopedia of Dolls
Vol I & II* (1968)
Darbyshire, L., (Ed.),
*The Collectors'
Encyclopedia of Toys
and Dolls* (1990)

King, C. E., *The
Encyclopedia of Toys*
(1978)
Miller, Martin and
Judith (Ed.),
*Miller's Antiques
Checklist – Dolls and
Teddy Bears* (1992)
Schoonmaker, P.,
*The Collector's
History of the Teddy
Bear* (1981)
Taylor, Kerry, *Letts
Guide to Collecting
Dolls* (1990)

OTHER COLLECTABLES

Baddiel, Sarah
Fabian, *The World
of Golf Collectables*
(1992)
Kay, Hilary, *Rock and
Roll Collectables*
(1992)
Kewley Charles & J.
Howard Farrar,
*Fishing Tackle for
Collectors* (1989)
Lambrou, Andreas,
*Fountain Pens
Vintage & Modern*
(1989)
Rolley, Claude, *Greek
Bronzes* (1986)
Turner, Anthony,
*Early Scientific
Instruments* (1987)
Turner, Gerard L E.,
*Nineteenth Century
Scientific Instruments*
(1983)

GLOSSARY

Acanthus Decorative leaf motif used to adorn a wide variety of objects.

Acid cutting A method of decorating glass where objects were coated with an acid-resistant substance, such as wax; a design was scratched on the wax with a steel point and fixed by dipping the object in acid.

Air twist stem On drinking glasses and other glassware, a stem decorated with spiral filaments of hollow glass.

Albarello A tin-glazed drug jar with a narrow waist.

Ambrotype A photograph made by exposing a glass plate treated with light-sensitive wet collodion. The negative was made positive by backing with black paper or paint (see p150).

Appliqué In textiles, applying small patches of fabric to a base fabric to make a design.

Arita An important centre for Japanese porcelain production, and a term used to describe one distinctive type of Japanese porcelain made in the area (see p67).

Armorial An engraved crest or coat of arms.

Arts & Craft A late 19th century artistic movement led by William Morris which advocated a return to medieval standards of crafts-manship and simplicity of design.

Automata A term covering a variety of mechanical toys with moving parts, popular during the 18th and 19th centuries.

Baluster Vase-shaped form with a bulbous base, narrow waist and slightly flared neck. Commonly used on silverwares, ceramics and stems of drinking glasses.

Ball and claw A furniture foot in the shape of an animal's paw grasping on ball. Used on cabriole legs.

Basaltes Unglazed black stoneware, developed by Wedgwood.

Bergère French style armchair with wood frame and upholstered sides.

Berlin Woolwork Amateur embroidery using coloured wools on a canvas grid.

Biscuit Unglazed porcelain, fired only once.

Blue-dash charger A delftware dish decorated with a border of blue brush strokes.

Blueing A decorative heat treatment applied to metal weapons which also protected from rust.

Bone china Porcelain made by the addition of large quantities of bone ash.

Bracket clock A type of spring-driven clock, designed to stand on a surface.

Britannia metal An alloy of tin, antimony and copper, used during the 19th century as a substitute for pewter.

Cabriole leg A furniture leg in the shape of an elongated S.

Cameo glass Wares made by combining two or more layers of differently coloured glass which was carved to made a design in relief.

Carriage clock A small portable clock with a carrying handle (see p110).

Case furniture Furniture intended as a receptacle, such as a chest of drawers.

Chasing A method of decorating silver and other metals by creating a raised pattern using a hammer or punch. Also known as embossing.

Chinoiserie European Oriental-style figures and scenes used to decorate many different types of object.

Creamware Creamy-white earthenware.

Cornice The projecting moulding at the top of tall furniture.

Credenza A long side-cabinet with glazed or solid doors.

Cross-banding A veneered edge at right-angles to the main veneer (see p44).

Cruet A frame for holding casters and bottles containing condiments.

Davenport A small writing desk with a sloped top above a case of drawers.

Delftware Tin-glazed earthenware from England or the Low Countries.

Dial The "face" of a clock, which shows the time.

Distressed A term used to describe an object that has been artificially aged.

Drum table A circular-topped table with a frieze containing drawers and supported by a central pedestal.

Ebonized Stained black in imitation of ebony.

Étui A small case for scissors and other small implements.

Faïence Tin-glazed earthenware from France.

Façon de Venise Glassware imitating Venetian styles.

Flatback Ceramic portrait figures with flat, undecorated backs, designed to stand against a wall or on a mantelpiece (see p81).

Flatware Any flat or shallow tableware, such as plates or cutlery.

Gesso A plaster-like substance used as a substitute for carved wood, or as a base for painted or gilded decoration.

Hallmark The marks stamped on silver or gold objects when passed at assay (the test for quality).

Hard-paste porcelain Porcelain made using the ancient Chinese combination of kaolin and petuntse.

Imari A type of Japanese porcelain with opulent decoration inspired by brocade designs, exported through the port of Imari.

Intaglio Incised gemstone or any incised decoration; the opposite of carving in relief.

Istoriato Narrative scenes painted on Italian *maiolica*.

Jacobite glass Wine glasses engraved with symbols of the Jacobites (supporters of Prince Charles Edward Stuart's claim to the throne).

Japanning European imitation of Oriental lacquer (see p58).

Jasperware A hard fine-grained stoneware decorated with high relief medallions, developed by Wedgwood.

Joined Term used to describe furniture made by a joiner.

Kakiemon Sparsely-decorated Japanese porcelain made by the Kakiemon family in the 17th century. The style was much imitated by later potters.

Kaolin A fine white granite clay used in hard-paste porcelain, also known as China clay.

Kashan Rug-making centre in Southern Iran, noted for high quality products.

Kazak Rugs from central Caucasus, usually decorated with distinctive geometric designs.

Kelim A flat woven rug with no pile.

Kneehole desk A writing desk with drawers on either side and a central recess for the user's legs.

Ladder back A country chair with a back made from a series of horizontal bars between the two vertical uprights.

Ladik A Turkish prayer rug, usually decorated with a niche and stylized tulip flowers.

Lap joint In silverware, the technique used to join a spoon finial to the stem by cutting each piece in opposing L-shapes.

Lead Crystal Glass containing lead oxide which gives extra weight and brilliance.

Library table A rectangular table with frieze drawers, end supports and a central stretcher.

Linen chest A hybrid coffer/chest of drawers, which may have both drawers and a lift-up top.

loaded In silverware, a hollow object (often a candlestick) which has been filled with pitch to give weight.

lock The firing mechanism of a gun.

long arm A firearm with a long barrel.

longcase clock A tall clock with a case containing weights and pendulum and hood housing dial and movement.

Lowboy A small dressing table, often with a single frieze drawer flanked by a deeper drawer.

Maiolica Tin-glazed earthenwares from Italy.

Majolica Enamelled stoneware with high relief decoration developed by Minton in the 19th century.

Marquetry Design formed from veneers of differently coloured woods.

Marriage The joining together of two previously unrelated parts to form a whole.

Mihrab A niche with a pointed arch, seen on prayer rugs.

Millefiori Glass made by fusing differently coloured rods of glass which resembles "a thousand flowers"; used for paperweights.

Monteith Large silver bowl, with a shallow scalloped rim.

Mortise and tenon Type of joint used in furniture; the mortise is a cavity, into which the shaped tenon fits and is held in place by dowels.

Mother-of-pearl Slices of shell often used for decorative inlay.

Motif A decorative detail, often repeated to form a pattern.

Moulded glass Glasswares manufactured in large quantities by forcing glass into a mould.

Mystery clock A clock of novel form in which the movement is ingeniously disguised.

Nailsea A factory near Bristol famous for novelty glass objects.

Occasional table Small, easily portable table.

Octant Device made from one eighth of a circle, used for measuring angular distance.

Opaque twist A white or coloured twist of glass contained in the stem of a drinking glass.

Ormolu Gilded bronze or brass; term also sometimes loosely used to describe any yellow-coloured metal.

Overglaze A second glaze laid over a first and refired; also known as enamelling.

Pad foot On furniture, a rounded foot, resembling that of an animal.

Palmette A stylized palm-leaf motif, often used to decorate Oriental carpets and furniture.

Papier mâché Paper pulp combined with glue, used to make small objects such as boxes and trays; also applied over a metal frame to make larger pieces of furniture, such as tables and chairs.

Parcel gilt Wood that has been partly gilded.

Parian Fine white biscuit porcelain resembling marble; popular from mid-19th century.

Parquetry Decorative veneers of wood laid in a geometric pattern.

Pate The Crown of a doll's head.

Patina The term used to describe the surface colour and sheen of furniture and silver which is built up from years of use and careful polishing.

Petuntse China stone; a granite used to make hard paste porcelain.

Plate A generic term for gold and silver vessels, not to be confused with Sheffield Plate or plated wares.

Porringer A two-handled dish, sometimes with a lid, originally for holding porridge or broth. Made from silver and pewter.

Pressed glass Glass wares formed by mechanical pressure applied to molten glass in a mould.

Quadrant A quarter circle, marked with degrees of a circle and with a weighted line or pointer, used as a navigational aid.

Quarter-veneered Four pieces of identical veneer, which are laid opposite each other to create a decorative effect.

Quartetto tables A set of four graduating matching tables, that can be stored inside each other.

Rack The structure, comprising several shelves, at the top of some dressers.

Refectory table Term used to describe the long rectangular dining tables of the 17th century and later.

Reproduction A piece which is a copy of an earlier design.

"Right" Dealers' term for something which is genuine and authentic, as opposed to "wrong", which means it is faked, altered or restored.

Sabre A curving sword used mainly by cavalrymen.

Sabre leg An elegant outward curving leg, associated with Regency furniture.

Salt A dish or cellar designed for holding salt.

Sampler Needlework pictures; incorporating different stitches and designs.

Scent bottle A small portable flask, often of flattened pear shape.

Sconce A plate or bracket on the wall to which lights or candle-holders could be attached. Also used to describe the wall lights themselves.

Settle A long wooden seat with a back and arms, and possibly a box seat.

Sextant Navigational instrument, formed from one sixth of a circle.

Sgrafitto Decorative technique whereby the surface has been scratched or incised to show a contrasting colour beneath; used mainly on ceramics and glass.

Shako A 19th century military cap of conical or cylindrical shape with a peak.

Shiraz Centre of distribution in central Iran for nomadic rugs decorated with simple geometric designs.

Slip Clay mixed with water, often used to decorate pottery.

Snuffer Cone-shaped metal implement used to extinguish candles.

Sterling silver Silver of at least 925 parts per 1000 purity. The minimum standard for English silver.

Stock The wooden part of a firearm to which the metal barrel and firing mechanism are attached.

Tester Wooden canopy over a bed, it may cover only half the bed and be supported by two or four posts; hence full tester or half tester beds.

Train A set of cog wheels and pinions in a clock movement.

Treen Small wooden domestic objects, sometimes in the shape of fruit.

Tunbridge ware Objects decorated with pictures or designs made from bundles of differently coloured wood cut in sections.

Tureen A large bowl on a foot used for serving soup.

Turned furniture Pieces made by turning on a lathe.

Veneer A thin sheet of wood applied to furniture for decorative effect.

Vesta case A small box used to contain vestas – early matches.

Vinaigrette A small portable container containing a sponge scented with vinegar.

Warp Threads used to make the foundation of a carpet running from one end of the carpet to the other and form the fringes.

Weft Cross wise threads, which run at right angles to the warp.

Wet plate camera Earliest form of camera, often made from brass-bound mahogany.

Whatnot Tall stand of four or five display shelves and sometimes a drawer in the base.

Windsor chair Country chair, usually with a saddle seat, hoop back and simple turned legs.

Wine funnel Cone, with a spout and often a matching dish for filtering and decanting wine.

Wing chair Upholstered chair with a high back and wing-like side projections.

X-frame The X-shaped construction of some chairs and stools.

INDEX

ACKNOWLEDGMENTS

The publishers would like to thank the following auction houses, museums, dealers, collectors and other sources for supplying pictures for use in this book.
Cover tCSK, clCSK, ctCSK, crSO, cSP, bRD; 2vaseSL, spoonCS, figuresCL, paperweight CL, longcaseSL, shoes CNY, clockSL, vaseSL, tobyjugCSK, chairSL, tureenSL, bureauCL, rug SL; 3bowlSL, trainsCSK, dollSL, casterSL, stool SL, glassCL; 10P; 11SL, 12 CSK; 13tCSK, bB; 14B; 15 B; 16L; 17AP; 18P; 19P; 20 NEC; 21P; 22tP, blBY, br P; 26KSA; 27CC; 28B; 29 B; 32DS; 34WD; 35SR; 36 SP; 37CL; 41MB; 42tSL, bWB; 43JGM; 44SL; 45 tSL, bLB; 46rWB; 47tl WB, cHum, blWB, brLB; 50PJ; 51cRen, bWB; 52SL; 53tMB, ctWB, cbJGM, bHum; 54tlSL, trSL, cl SL, blSL, 55SL; 56bWB; 57tWil, cSL, bHock; 58bl RD, rSL; 59blLB, rSL; 60 tlCL, clWak; 61ISL, cWB, bCL; 62S; 63ICL, rCL; 65 tCL; 66SL, blSL, brCSK; 67cSL, brSL; 68 lCNY, cSL, rCNY; 69 lCL, cSL, rCL; 70lSL; 71SL; 72ISL, rCL, bcSL; 75tSL, crSZ; 74clCL, cr SL, bCL; 75tx2SL; 76tCL, bSL; 77CL; 78tCSK, 79 cMB; 80tMB, cSL, bSNY; 81ISL, cMB, rDen; 84tlCNY, cCNY, bcCNY; 85SLx2; 86lCL, rCNY; 87tSL, clCNY, crCNY; 88cSL, blCNY, cbSL, rbSL; 89 CNY; 90ctSL, clCL, bSL; 91cSL, crCNY, blCNY; 92CSKx3, bcMB; 93

CNYx3; 94ISB, rCL; 95tl SL, cSB, bCS; 96CL; 97 clCL, crSL; 98lCL, rSL; 99SLx2; 100CL; 101 tlH&G, crSL, bSL; 102 SLx2bcCL; 103SL; bx3 CNY; 106lSL; ctSO, crSL; 107SO; 108cAW, crSL; 109SL; 110SLx3; 111lCL, rSL, brDR; 113lSNY, rSNY, bSNY; 114lCL, rCL; 115lCl, rCL, bSL; 116 SLx2; 117cSl, bSNY; 118 tCL, bSL; 119tlCL, trPS, bCL; 120 lSL, rCNY, rbCNY; 121 Bx5; 122ISL, rRC, bCL; 123cCl, bCL; 124tr SL. clSL, crCL; 125 lCNY, cCL, rCNY; 126 lSL, 127ISL, rPC, bB; 128 lSLx2, bPS; 129cCSK, bSNY; 131ISL, clCSK, crSL, rCSK; 132SLx2; 133 cSP, bSL; 134SPx3; 135 cSP, bDA; 136CL; 137 rCL, cCL, bMaB; 138t SL, cCSK, bSL; 139 rSL, cCNY; 140CSK; 141 CSKx3; 142CSKx2, bSL; 143CSKx3; 144SL; 145tCNY, cSL, bWAL; 146lSL, rSL; 147rPS, cCL, bPS; 148CLx2; 149CLx3; 150MB; 151CSKx3; 152 CSKx2; 153CSKx4; 154 SBx2; 155t&cSB, bSNY; 156l, c, rCSK, blSL; 157B; 158brB, trCL; 159cl, crCSK, bSL; 160BY

Key
t top, c centre, b bottom, l left, r right

AP Adrian Stemp Antiques, Brighton
AW Anthony Woodburn, Leigh, Kent
B Bonhams
BY Bermondsey Market
CC The Clock Clinic, Lower Richmond Rd; London

CL Christie's London
CNY Christie's New York
CS Christie's Scotland
CSK Christie's South Kensington
DA Dottie Ayers
Den Richard Dennis, Ilminster
DR Derek Roberts, Tonbridge, Kent
DS Dennis Severs, Folgate Street, London
H&G Hope & Glory, Kensington Church Street, London
Hock William Hockley Antiques, Petworth, West Sussex
Hum Humphry Antiques, Petworth, West Sussex
JGM John G. Morris Ltd, Petworth, West Sussex
KSA Keith Skeel Antiques, Islington High Street, London
LB Lesley Bragge Antiques, Petworth, West Sussex
MaB Mint and Boxed, London
MB Mitchell Beazley
NEC British International Antiques Fair, Birmingham
P Portobello Road
PC Phillips, Cardiff
PJ Patrick Jefferson Antiques, 572 Kings Road, London
PS Phillips, London
RC Royal Copenhagen
RD Richard Davidson Antiques, Arundel, West Sussex
Ren Rendall Antiques, London
SB Sotheby's Billingshurst
SL Sotheby's London
SNY Sotheby's New York

SO Strike One, 33 Balcombe St, London
SP Sue Pearson Antiques, 13 1/2 Prince Albert Street; Brighton
SR Sotheby's Restoration Department
SZ Sotheby's Zurich
Wak Michael Wakelin and Helen Linfield, Petworth, West Sussex
WAL Wallis & Wallis, Lewes, Sussex
WB William Bedford PLC, London
WD West Dean College, West Sussex
Wil T. G. Wilkinson Antiques, Petworth, West Sussex

Special photography p10-34 Jacqui Hurst and Ian Booth
Illustrations by Karen Cochrane, John Hutchinson, Simon Miller and Vanessa Luff

Special thanks are also due to the following specialists for their help in the preparation of this book:
Furniture Richard Davidson
Pottery and Porcelain Gordon Lang, Eric Knowles
Silver and metalware John Wilson
Glass Eric Knowles
Clocks John Mighell
Rugs, Carpets, Textiles Joanna Macfarlane
Art Nouveau, Art Deco Eric Knowles
Dolls and Bears Sue Pearson
Rock and Pop, Film Memorabilia Carey Wallace
Other Collectables Alex Crum-Ewing
Tribal Kevin Conru